MW00947215

<u>A JOURNEY THROUGH A DREAM</u>

Written by

JOE SILVA

Based on a true story, 'A JOURNEY THROUGH A DREAM' is a remarkable tale of a talented musician who dedicates his life to following his dream of making it big in the music industry. He is determined to do whatever it takes to reach the top, but he is not willing to compromise his moral values to achieve his goal. After a series of unforeseen disappointments, personal setbacks, financial struggles, and heart-break, he finds that he has hit rock-bottom. Miraculously, on the eve of becoming homeless, the young dream-seeker receives a revelation after reaching deep inside of his soul & faith and pleading a personal cry for help. Within minutes, he comes eye-to-eye with an unexpected, yet unmistakable angel on earth, who propels him back onto the track of his dream.

"'A JOURNEY THROUGH A DREAM' is a cross between 'The Wizard of Oz' & 'The Jazz Singer'."
- Industry Insider

"I met Joe Silva on the set of 'Married... with Children' in the 90's and we've remained close friends ever since. We've cheered each other on during our accomplishments and picked each other up when times were tough. Joe refuses to give up on his dreams, and his life is richer for that, as are the lives of those all around him. He remains true and never compromises his moral values throughout his journey within an extremely competitive entertainment industry."
- Steven Ritt (Hollywood Animal Trainer & Film Director)

"Joe Silva is one of the few, true, shoot-from-the-hip songwriters of our time."
- Will Lee (Late Show w/ David Letterman Bassist)

"I met Joe Silva at Sun Studio several years ago. I liked him immediately! He was interested and interesting! I've kept up with him through the years. He's tireless. Always after a story and a song. He's a modern day Troubadour. I love his love for his work. He's the real deal. He's a great songwriter and much much more! I'm a huge fan. Keep movin' Joe. You do it so well!"
- Jimmy Tittle (Johnny Cash Bassist & Son-in-Law)

"Joe Silva is a melodic and thoughtful songwriter. Alarm fans are going to love Joe."
- Mike Peters (Songwriter & Lead Singer of The Alarm)

"A great screenplay that a lot of musicians will be able to relate to, whether they made it or not because whether any of us made it or not the path to success or failure in this business is basically the same for all of us... it's just that some of us got a "yes" that worked out, most of us got the word "no" tossed as us multiple times and it's right there that a "struggling musician" has to be their strongest... working through the "no" responses while you continue and NEVER GIVE UP searching for a "Yes!" and then ensuring it's the right "Yes!". If you can do this and die whether you got the "yes" or you got all negatives then you are a true musician. Joe is definitely one of the true musicians."
- Bob Cowsill (Songwriter & Singer of The Cowsills band)

"Joe Silva came into my life and sent up a flare, igniting a light to remind me to never give up on my dreams. He is my pal, partner, confidant, inspiration, cheerleader, and my best friend. Because of him that river is still flowing! Oh yeah... and he is a great writer too!"
- Nancy Priddy (Actress/Singer: Bewitched, The Waltons, Leonard Cohen, Bitter End Singers)

"I've known Joe for many years and his passion for music and life is inspirational. He is a terrific songwriter, instrumentalist and vocalist whose songs are created through and by his life experiences."
- Loren Harriet (Sports Emmy Award Winner & Latin Grammy Nominated Music Producer)

"Where you running to?" **- B.B. King**
"As far as my music will take me, Mr. King." **- Joe Silva**
"Well, there you'll go!" **- B.B. King**

'A Journey Through A Dream' is written in a movie screen-play format. It is designed such that the reader becomes the "Movie Director" in their mind while experiencing this literary format. Each scene is briefly described, with all of the pertinent information given, along with the complete dialogue. It is up to the reader's imagination to color and detail each setting, form each character's expressions and accents, while absorbing and delivering the meaning of every intended message throughout this tale.

Uniquely, this book has a 19-song soundtrack that is musically integral and relevant throughout the story. Titled the same name as the book, it may be ordered through Amazon.com or downloaded via music websites such as iTunes. Search 'Joe Silva A Journey Through A Dream'. The soundtrack was co-produced by 'Late Show w/ David Letterman' drummer, Anton Fig, and includes several members of the Late Show band, Ace Frehley of the rock band 'KISS', James Stevenson of The Cult & The Alarm, and over a dozen more musical notables from around the world. It was recorded at Abbey Road Studios in London, Sun Studio in Memphis, Foo Fighters' 606 Studio in Los Angeles, and Anton Fig's Lion Head Studio in New York.

While combining the reading of the book with the listening of the soundtrack, this audio and literary experience should last the length of a full-feature movie. Each time the reader journeys through the full experience, a different "movie" is realized, based on the participant's imagination at the time.

Throughout the story, the script is kept to Hollywood screenplay standards, including layout, the original type-writer font and page size. For those not familiar with screenplays, you will catch on quickly. Character Dialogue is always centered on the page. Scene Intros and details, as well as Character Intros, are justified to the left side of the page (INT means Interior shot, EXT means Exterior shot). Camera/Editing direction is given on the right side of the page (Fade-to, Cut-to, etc.)

Soundtrack Song Lyrics may be found at the end of this book.

?

A JOURNEY THROUGH A DREAM

STORY & MUSIC BY:

JOE SILVA

www.TheJoeSilvaWebsite.com

Joe Silva
PO Box 7553
Cumberland, RI 02864

FADE IN:

INT. CHILDREN'S BEDROOM (CIRCA 1969) - MORNING

3-year-old Joe gets up from bed and walks over to look at
his newborn sister in her crib on the other side of the
room. He glances back at the large full jar of orange baby
aspirins on the dresser that he can just about reach.
Walking over to it, he opens the container and begins to
devour the pills, with an obvious look that he is enjoying
the candy-tasting nature of them. Once the bottle is empty,
he looks at the seven pills still in his hand, looks at his
baby sister, and throws 4 back into the container, then
leaves the cap on his bed while exchanging it for the toy
drum and sticks that he sleeps with every night. He then
exists the room.

                                        CUT TO:

INT. LIVING ROOM - MOMENTS LATER

Joe sits on a small chair, too close to the television set,
playing his drum to a song that is being sung on 'Sesame
Street'. His sister Jade enters the room, holding the near-
empty jar of aspirin.

JADE, 10-year-old girl, wearing pajamas

                    JADE
               (Speaking in a loud
               whisper)
          Joey... Joey...

Joe continues playing, not hearing his sister over the TV
and his drumming. Jade taps him on the shoulder, startling
Joe, who stops playing.

JOE, a 3-year-old boy, also wearing pajamas

                    JOE
          What?

                    JADE
          Did you eat all of the pills that
          were inside of this jar?

                    JOE
          No.

                    JADE
          Are you sure?

                                        (CONTINUED)

CONTINUED:

                    JOE
                (nervously)
        No, I didn't eat all of them.

                    JADE
        Well if you did, and you aren't
        telling me the truth, all of those
        pills in your tummy are going to make
        you die.

Joe drops his drum sticks and begins to cry. Jade runs out
of the room, calling for their father.

                                    FADE TO:

INT. HOSPITAL HALLWAY - LATER

Joe is being quickly whisked in a panic on a gurney toward
an operating room. An emergency worker begins to speak with
Joe's father.

                    EMERGENCY WORKER
        I'm sorry, but we can't allow parents
        into the room while the child's
        stomach is being pumped.

                    JOE
        GUS! I WANT GUS!! I WANT GUS!!

                    EMERGENCY WORKER
        Who is Gus? He might be hallucinating
        from the overdose.

JOE'S FATHER, Tall middle-aged conservative man. Looks like
an Insurance Salesman.

                    JOE'S FATHER
        That's me. He sometimes calls me by
        my first name. Can't I just go in and
        hold his hand?

                    EMERGENCY WORKER
        I'm sorry sir.

Operating room door closes as one more, muffled, "GUS!" is
shouted from Joe's mouth.

                                    FADE TO:

INT. BACK IN THE CHILDRENS' BEDROOM - EVENING

Joe's father walks into the room where Joe is already laying in his bed.

> JOE'S FATHER
> Hey Big Joe

> JOE
> (Groggy voice)
> Hey Big Gus

> JOE'S FATHER
> So, you sure learned an important lesson today, right?

> JOE
> Uh- Huh

> JOE'S FATHER
> Please promise me that you'll never do that again.

> JOE
> I promise, Dad. Can I have my drum please?

Joe's father finds the drum on the floor and gives it to his son.

> JOE'S FATHER
> I'm not sure where the sticks are, but you can find them in the morning. You are getting to be a good little drummer boy. What do you figure, Joe, success?

> JOE
> What does sucress mean?

> JOE'S FATHER
> No - Suc-Cess... It means when you work really hard at something and you get what you were working for. I can say that you are successful at playing that drum, because you worked at learning how to play it.

> JOE
> It doesn't feel like work. It feels like fun.

(CONTINUED)

CONTINUED:

>   JOE'S FATHER
> Then that means you are even MORE
> successful. What do you figure, Joe?

>   JOE
> Sucress

>   JOE'S FATHER
> Success... Did you say your prayers
> yet?

>   JOE
> I said them with Mom.

>   JOE'S FATHER
> OK. Good night, then. I love you.

>   JOE
> Yep. Good night Dad.

Joe's father leaves the room, not quite closing the door all the way. An argument ensues almost instantly between Joe's father and mother (over who's fault it was that the aspirins were accessible to Joe earlier in the day). Joe is seen looking frightened, yet familiar with the quarreling sound. He turns to lay on his side and pulls the covers over his head.

>   FADE TO:

INT. THEATER STAGE - LATE MORNING (10 YEARS LATER)

The theater is empty aside from a panel of judges sitting in the first row of seats, holding clipboards. It is audition day for the snare drummer position in this year's Rhode Island All State Concert Band. A snare drum is set-up toward the front of the stage, and a young drummer is reading the sheet music on the music stand as he plays the drum for the judges. Joe is next in line to audition, and there are a dozen more drumming hopefuls standing in line behind him. The drummer ahead of Joe completes the musical piece and walks off the stage, and Joe nervously takes his position at the drum and sheet of music.

>   JUDGE
> Please loudly and clearly state your
> name, school, and music teacher that
> recommended you.

>   JOE
> Joseph Silva... South Cumberland
> Middle School... Mr. Durago.

CONTINUED:

> **JUDGE**
> Thank you. The musical piece that you
> will audition with is 'Ode To Joy',
> which you will find there on the
> music stand. You may take a moment to
> adjust the drum and music stand.

> **JOE**
> Oh, that's OK. I know that there are
> a lot of other drummers behind me
> that still need to audition, so I
> will start right in on the piece to
> save some time.

The judges begin to write onto their clipboards, and Joe
starts drumming. At one point he hits the rim of the drum,
but other than that he plays the piece perfectly.

> **JUDGE**
> Thank you, Joseph. We will be
> contacting Mr. Durago this week with
> the audition results.

> **JOE**
> Thank you.

Joe walks out of the building with his drum sticks and gets
into a car where his father has been waiting for him.

> **JOE (cont'd)**
> Sorry that was so long, Dad. There
> must have been fifteen drummers ahead
> of me.

> **JOE'S FATHER**
> No problem. What do you figure?

> **JOE**
> Success... I think I played the piece
> really well.

> DISSOLVE TO:

INT. SOUTH CUMBERLAND MIDDLE SCHOOL HALLWAY - MORNING (ONE
WEEK LATER)

Students are milling about in the hallway as they make their
way to their classes. The school's music teacher, Mr.
Durago, tracks down Joe as he exchanges books in his locker.

CONTINUED:

MR. DURAGO, Middle School Music Teacher and Band Director

> MR. DURAGO
> Joe! Good... I found you. I have some
> great news.

> JOE
> I'm the All-State drummer?!

> MR. DURAGO
> Close. You are the runner-up.

> JOE
> Well, how is that good news?

> MR. DURAGO
> Are you kidding me? That is quite an
> accomplishment. All of the best
> drummers from the entire state were
> auditioning for that musical
> position. You should feel very proud
> of yourself.

Mr. Durago hands the runner-up medal to Joe, who places it
on his locker shelf without looking at it and closes the
door in disappointment.

> MR. DURAGO (cont'd)
> Do you want to know why you didn't
> come in first?

> JOE
> (sounding deflated)
> Sure.

> MR. DURAGO
> It was because you were too nice, and
> I admire that.

> JOE
> I don't understand.

> MR. DURAGO
> The judges wrote that you didn't
> adjust the drum so it would be at the
> correct angle for your playing
> because you were concerned for all
> the other drummers that were waiting
> for their turn, which resulted in you
> hitting the rim once instead of the
> drum head.

CONTINUED:

                    JOE
          Live and learn, I guess. Well, I'm
          going to be late for class. Thanks
          for the medal, Mr. Durago.

                    MR. DURAGO
          You earned that medal... and yes,
          live and learn, but never stop being
          nice to others, no matter what.

                                        FADE TO:

INT. JOE'S HOUSE (CIRCA 1977) - MORNING

Christmas morning. Joe's family is just waking up, and he is
walking down the hall, wearing one of his several KISS rock-
band t-shirts, when he is greeted by his younger sister.

LEE, Joe's younger sister.

                    LEE
                  (Excited)
          Joe! Good! You're up. Go wake up Dad.
          Everyone else is in the living room
          waiting to open presents.

Joe turns around and walks down the hall, opens the farthest
door and looks in.

                    JOE
          Dad? Hmmm.

Joe walks toward the living room where everyone is assembled
(4 sisters and his mother). His mother's eyes look puffy
from crying.

                    JOE (cont'd)
          Dad isn't in his bed.

JOE'S MOTHER, Middle-aged woman wearing a robe.

                    JOE'S MOTHER
          Check the basement.

                    JOE
          Why the basement?

                    JOE'S MOTHER
          Just check the basement.

                                        (CONTINUED)

CONTINUED:

Joe quickly makes his way down the stairs, finding his
father asleep on a couch. Joe's snare drum and drum seat are
set-up in the middle of the room next to a pile of records
and a record player.

                    JOE
          Dad?... Dad wake up. It is Christmas!

Joe's father gives a slight snore. Joe walks over to his
snare drum, picks up his sticks and begins to play lightly.
His father starts to wake up.

                    JOE'S FATHER
          Wha... what?

Joe stops playing.

                    JOE
          Merry Christmas, Dad. Why are you
          down here and not in your bed?

                    JOE'S FATHER
          Oh... umm... I figured I'd get out of
          Santa's way so he could set-up your
          Christmas present near the tree.

                    JOE
          Set-up?

                    JOE'S FATHER
          Come on... let's go open presents.

                                        CUT TO:

INT. LIVING ROOM - MOMENTS LATER

Most of the presents have been opened. There are piles of
wrapping paper and new toys scattered all over the room. A
Christmas tree is lit up, and there is something bulky near
it under a large sheet.

                    JADE
          What is under the sheet?

                    JOE'S FATHER
          Well, let's take a look.

Joe's father walks over to the sheet and reads a tag that is
pinned to it.

CONTINUED:

                    JOE'S FATHER (cont'd)
          It says "To Big Joe - Always march to
          the beat of your own drums!"

Joe leaps up in excitement and slowly removes the sheet,
revealing a slightly beat-up drum set (the drum-wrapping is
un-peeling from a drum or two, and the cymbals are slightly
warped)

                    JOE
          WOW!! A full drum-set!! Thank you SO
          much Mom & Dad!

                    JOE'S MOTHER
          It is from Santa.

                    JOE
          Yeah, right. I can't wait to play it!

                    JOE'S FATHER
          Actually, you have your music teacher
          at school to thank. He helped us find
          a drum-set that we could afford
          through a friend of his. He told me
          that if you do as well on the full
          drum-set that you do on the snare
          drum in the school band, that you'll
          be writing out your own checks
          someday.

                    JOE
          Yeah, Mr. Durago is really nice. He
          has been teaching me some guitar and
          piano, too, during home-room periods.
          He knows that I want to write my own
          songs and said that learning the
          basics of those instruments will be
          important. He plays in a band at
          night. He's really cool. Maybe
          someday I'll get to play for KISS!

                    JADE
          Well, if YOU ever start a band, or
          join KISS, I'll be at every show.

                    JOE'S FATHER
          What do you figure, Joe?

                    JOE
          Success!

                                        FADE TO:

INT. LARGE SCHOOL AUDITORIUM - EARLY EVENING - SIX MONTHS
LATER

The South Cumberland Middle School auditorium is packed with
parents and students, who are assembled to watch the final
concert of the Middle School Concert Band, which is
performing on the stage. Joe makes his way from the line of
snare drums at the back of the stage to a drum-set that is
positioned off to the side toward the front of the stage.
The band director introduces the final song of the concert.

                    MR. DURAGO
          It has been a pleasure for me to work
          with all of these fine young student
          musicians over the past few years.
          For our last number, I'd like to
          feature the talent of our lead
          drummer, Joe, performing on full
          drum-set. This is 'Ode To Joy'.

Mr. Durago raises his conductor wand, looks over at Joe and
gives a certain smile & nod, as if he is about to let the
world in on a secret that he has been holding inside, then
his hand drops as he fervently begins the orchestra in on
the piece of music.

The band performs the classical piece in a traditional
style, while Joe weaves through and around the piece with
hints of jazz & rock style playing. Audience members react
by becoming more alert and adjusting themselves in their
seats to get a better view of the young musician's drumming.
The song ends to a roaring standing ovation. As the band
members mill about in search of their parents, Joe finds Mr.
Durago in a wing of the stage before leaving the auditorium.

                    JOE
          Mr. Durago...

Joe extends his hand for a handshake.

                    JOE (cont'd)
          Thank you so much for everything that
          you've done for me. I'm really going
          to miss playing in the school band.

                    MR. DURAGO
          The pleasure was all mine, Joe. You
          are one fine player, and an
          outstanding kid. I'm sure that you'll
          enjoy playing with the high school
          band in the Fall, too.

(CONTINUED)

CONTINUED:

                    JOE
          Well, I won't actually be playing in
          the high school band, Mr. Durago. As
          you know, I've put a band together
          with some friends from school. I was
          able to book us a few shows over the
          summer at a nightclub. I convinced
          the club-owner that even though we
          are only kids, we are probably good
          enough to stand-up to the other bands
          that play there. He gave us every
          other Tuesday night to start with.
          We'll play cover songs until I write
          enough of my own music to go entirely
          original. You can't make it to the
          top by playing other peoples' songs,
          right?

Mr. Durago reaches behind a section of the theater curtain
and picks up a battered acoustic guitar case, handing it to
Joe.

                    MR. DURAGO
          I thought you might say that. Here...
          this will help you to write those
          songs.

                    JOE
          But, Mr. Durago, I couldn't possibly
          accept your guitar.

                    MR. DURAGO
          I was planning on picking up a new
          one for myself this summer anyway.
          Besides, I can't think of any student
          that I've ever had who was more
          determined to "make-it" in the music
          industry than you... Now go out into
          the world and make me proud.

Joe switches the guitar case handle from his right hand to
his left hand and gives Mr. Durago a firm hand shake.

                    JOE
          I sure will make you proud. I
          promise. Thanks for everything.

Joe makes his way down the stage stairs to a crowd of
admiring parents and class-mates.

                                        FADE TO:

INT. BATHROOM AT JOE'S HOUSE - LATER THAT EVENING

Joe is in the shower, humming the melody of 'Ode To Joy', when he hears a knock on the door and his father enters. Joe peers around the shower curtain to see that it's his Dad that came into the bathroom, then continues to shower.

                    JOE
          What's up, Dad?

                    JOE'S FATHER
          What do you figure, Joe?

                    JOE
          Success.

                    JOE'S FATHER
          That was one heck of a performance
          that you gave tonight.

                    JOE
          Thanks. I was nervous at first during
          the last song when the drums were set
          up at the edge of the stage, but then
          I just felt so energized by being in
          front of the audience like that. I
          want to talk to you and Mom tonight
          about me playing at a nightclub this
          summer.

                    JOE'S FATHER
          Actually, I've got some news to tell
          you right now... You know that your
          mother and I haven't been getting
          along for quite some time, and I will
          be leaving home tonight.

Joe peers around the shower curtain again, with suds in his hair.

                    JOE
          What do you mean?

                    JOE'S FATHER
          I'm sorry, Joe. I hope that you'll
          understand someday. Maybe we can see
          each other next weekend. Please know
          that I love you.

Joe's father leaves the bathroom.

                    JOE
          What??

                                        (CONTINUED)

CONTINUED:

Joe vigorously attempts to rinse the suds out of his hair so he can dry up, get dressed, and talk to his father before he leaves. While drying up, he hears his sisters and mother crying from his parent's bedroom. He gets dressed and joins them on the large bed that his parents once shared, and Joe begins to cry, too.

> JOE'S MOTHER
> (Shouting)
> Listen to your children crying! Why
> are you doing this!?

The door slams, making the girls cry even harder. Joe gets up and hurries to the living room window where he watches the headlights of his father's car pull out of the driveway. He runs downstairs, picks up his drum sticks, and begins to pound his drum-set heavily and frantically, displaying much hurt and anger. This goes on for a minute or so until he kicks his bass drum and a cymbal over, resulting in a loud crash... and then silence for a second before he places his face in his hands and cries uncontrollably.

> FADE TO:

EXT. DRIVEWAY / JOE'S MOTHER'S HOUSE - MORNING (LATER THAT SUMMER)

Joe and his four sisters are loading beach blankets and chairs into the trunk of an old beat-up looking Chevrolet. Joe's mother comes out of the house with a cooler to add to the load, and her kids begin to complain.

> LEE
> Mom, Joe called the front seat but I
> told you that I wanted to sit in the
> front.

> JOE
> You can have the front on the way
> back from the beach. No big deal.

> JADE
> I can't believe that THIS is the car
> we need to drive around in now.

DIANE, Joe's oldest sister, dressed more for a fashion show than the beach

> DIANE
> Car? More like a jalopy. It'll
> probably fall apart before we even
> get to the beach.

> (CONTINUED)

CONTINUED:

                    JOE'S MOTHER
          Listen! I'm working three jobs to
          feed you kids. I'm doing the best
          that I can. Now get in the car and do
          NOT ruin my beach day. I don't get
          another day off until two weeks from
          now.

Joe's mother tries to close the trunk, but it appears as
though it doesn't want to latch.

                    DIANE
          See?

Joe's mother gives an "If looks could kill" look at Diane
and slams the trunk lid closed. Everyone quietly gets into
the car.

                    JOE
          At least it has a good sound system.

                    JADE
          It's an eight-track tape player. They
          don't even make them anymore, so we
          are stuck listening to the one
          cassette that we have. Neil
          Diamond... Again!

                    DIANE
          Nope! I borrowed 'The Guess Who' from
          my friend Rick's van.

The Guess Who song, 'American Woman', begins blaring out of
the open windows as the Chevy jalopy rolls down the street.

                              DISSOLVE TO:

INT. JOE'S MOTHER'S CAR - LATE AFTERNOON

Neil Diamond's 'Forever in Blue Jeans' song is playing
softly through the speakers while Joe's mother drives home
from the beach. Joe listens from the back seat, awake and
sandwiched between his sleeping sisters.

                    JOE
          Mom, can you rewind it a bit to the
          part just before the chorus?

                    JOE'S MOTHER
          I'm not sure how to work the player
          that well.
                         (MORE)

                                        (CONTINUED)

CONTINUED:

> JOE'S MOTHER (cont'd)
> I'll just reset it to the beginning
> of the song. I'm surprised that you
> like Neil Diamond.

> JOE
> I can't get his songs out of my head
> once I hear them. That probably makes
> him a really good songwriter. I just
> want to figure out the transition
> that he and his band do right before
> the chorus.

The song starts over..."Money talks, but it don't sing and dance and it don't walk..."

> JOE (cont'd)
> Great lyrics.

> FADE TO:

EXT. DRIVEWAY / COUNTRY HOUSE - DAY (10 YEARS LATER)

Late model car pulls into the driveway of large country estate. Longer-haired rocker guy gets out of the car and walks to the door of the 19th Century Victorian home and rings the doorbell, looking somewhat nervous. Middle-aged woman opens door.

MRS. CROSS, Attractive middle-aged woman

> MRS. CROSS
> Oh, Hi Joe. Shelly is out shopping
> for some things for your trip to Los
> Angeles together. Are you excited?

JOE, Now a rock & roller, early 20's

> JOE
> (Speaking in a
> nervous tone)

> Hi Mrs. Cross. Yes, I am very
> excited. I knew Shelly was out, which
> is why I dropped by now. I'd like to
> speak with you and Mr. Cross. Is here
> here?

> MRS. CROSS
> (Giving a curious
> stare)

> Sure, come on in...

CONTINUED:

CUT TO:

INT. FOYER AREA WITH LARGE ORNATE STAIRCASE

                    MRS. CROSS
          Paul... Paul, Joe is here and he'd
          like to speak with us.

MR. CROSS, Tall middle-aged man

                    MR. CROSS
               (Descending down the
                staircase)
          Well, hello there Joe. What is going
          on?

                    JOE
          Hi Mr. Cross. I came here to speak
          with you and Mrs. Cross ahead of the
          trip that Shelly and I are making to
          Los Angeles in the morning. As you
          know, we have been together for 6
          years now, and I can't imagine loving
          anyone more than I do Shelly. I
          intend on giving her a diamond ring
          while we are away, and would like to
          ask you both for her hand in marriage
          before I propose to her.

                    MRS. CROSS
               (Smiling through
                tears and hugging
                Joe)
          What wonderful news! Of COURSE you
          have our blessings!! Right, Paul?

Mr. Cross extends a hand to Joe.

                    MR. CROSS
          Yes. Of course. You'll make a fine
          husband for our daughter. Should we
          open a bottle of wine?

                    JOE
          Thanks, but I'm not sure what time
          Shelly will be getting back here and
          I don't want to ruin the surprise.
          Plus, I have to play a late concert
          tonight so I should hold-off on any
          afternoon drinking to save my energy.
               (MORE)

(CONTINUED)

CONTINUED:

                     JOE (cont'd)
I'll request a rain-check, though,
and take you up on it with Shelly
when we return as an engaged couple
from L.A.

                     MR. CROSS
          (Chuckling his words)
That's IF she says "Yes"

                     MRS. CROSS
Of course she will say yes! I am so
happy right now, and will try to hide
it from Shelly when she gets back. It
won't be easy to keep this one a
secret. Have a fantastic trip, and
break a leg on stage tonight!

                     JOE
          (While leaving
           through the door)
I am very happy, too. Thank you both
so much. I'll see you next week.

EXT. THE LIVING ROOM MUSIC NIGHTCLUB - NIGHT

In the heart of Providence, Rhode Island, a line of people
are trying to get into the packed 'Living Room' music venue.
The marquis is lit up with letters spelling "TONIGHT - THE
THREATS"

                              DISSOLVE TO:

INT. BAND DRESSING ROOM

Joe's band-mates warm up, primp rock & roll hair, etc. While
Joe is huddled in corner with Shelly. They are holding hands
and finishing a prayer together when the stage manager walks
into the dressing room.

KEEBLER, STAGE MANAGER, Short & stocky in build, wearing
lots of backstage passes around his neck in laminates like a
trophy, holding a flashlight.

                     KEEBLER
          (Gravely voice)
Five minutes until showtime! Look at
ya's... You're way too pretty for
this place! Stop primping in front of
the mirror and tune your guitars!
I'll be leading you to the stage with
this flashlight.
          (MORE)

                              (CONTINUED)

CONTINUED:

                    KEEBLER (cont'd)
         The place is packed tonight! Lot's of
         girls that just want to get their
         hands all over your...
                   (Notices that Shelly
                    is in the corner of
                    the room with Joe)
         Oops... sorry Shelly. You know by now
         how some of these fans can be...

                    JOE
                   (Speaking softly to
                    Shelly)
         Don't listen to Keebler. Everyone is
         here for our music. Plus, I would
         never do anything to jeopardize our
         relationship... ever. OK? I've got to
         get to the stage, and Cindy is
         probably out there looking for you. I
         added her and her new boyfriend onto
         the guest-list. We should probably
         get out of here right after our show.
         The plane departs at 6:30 tomorrow
         morning.

SHELLY, Extremely pretty female in her early 20's, dressed
sexy yet classy

                    SHELLY
                   (Giving Joe a good-
                    luck kiss)
         Well, I doubt that Cindy's boyfriend
         is here. She told me earlier that he
         broke up with her. I feel so bad for
         her. They just never seem to work
         out... By the way, I know that you're
         all mine, and I ain't lettin' you
         go... Ever! Have a great show. I'll
         be out there singing along. I'll meet
         you back here after the last song. I
         Love you.

INT. MAIN MUSIC ROOM IN NIGHTCLUB

Joe and his band are on the stage and he is introducing the
last song of the concert.

                    JOE
         Thank you all so much for coming to
         our show tonight. This last song
         features David, my favorite guitar-
         slinger on the planet.
                   (MORE)

                                              (CONTINUED)

CONTINUED:

                    JOE (cont'd)
          This is Egyptian Love Song, and we
          are The Threats.

Joe and The Threats perform their last song, while the crowd
sings/shouts the title of the song, 'Egyptian Love Song',
each time it comes around in the chorus. The place is
packed, standing-room-only. Shelly is ignoring guys who are
trying to pick her up, while she talks over the music to her
best friend Cindy.

<PLAY SONG 'EGYPTIAN LOVE SONG'>

                    SHELLY
               (Slightly shouting
                over the loud music)
          This is Joe's last song. I've got to
          go.

CINDY, Short girl with a wild-side punk look

                    CINDY
               (Having a tough time
                hearing Shelly over
                the music)
          What?

                    SHELLY
               (Shouting louder)
          I've got to make my way back to the
          dressing room! This is the band's
          last song and we are leaving right
          after the show! Early flight!

                    CINDY
               (Giving a hug to
                Shelly)
          Have a BLAST in L.A.! I am SOOO
          jealous!!

                    SHELLY
          I'll find you a hot Hollywood actor
          boyfriend and fly you out there!

                    CINDY
               (Brushing Shelly away)
          Yeah, Yeah,... See you next week!

                                        (CONTINUED)

CONTINUED:

The band ends the song and Joe says his "thank you's" to the crowd while Shelly makes her way to the dressing room through the over-packed crowd. Camera cuts back and forth between Joe making his way through the same crowd while being hit-on by female fans, and Shelly trying to ignore guys offering her drinks as they both struggle to get through the mass of people. While squeezing by some people to get through the crowd, Joe runs into his sister.

JADE, conservatively dressed female in her late 20's

     JADE
  Joey! Great show!

     JOE
  Hey! Jade! I didn't think you could
  make it tonight. I would've added you
  to the guest-list.

     JADE
  Bill didn't have to work late after-
  all.

     JOE
  Where IS Bill?

     JADE
  Who knows?! Somewhere in this crowd.
  This place is packed tonight!

     JOE
  I know! I'm psyched! Hey, I feel bad
  that I can't talk long, but I told
  Shelly to meet me right after the
  show so we can get out of here for
  our trip. Did you see her?

     JADE
  Only from across the bar. She didn't
  see me, though. Does she have any
  idea?

     JOE
  I don't think so! Hey, next time you
  see me I'll most likely be an engaged
  man!

     JADE
  Have a great time, Joey!... and call
  me after she says "YES"!

     JOE
  I will!!

INT. BAND DRESSING ROOM

Joe is drying his sweat-soaked hair with a towel.

                    SHELLY
          You were SO great tonight! I don't
          know where you get all that energy
          from, but I hope that you saved some
          for me to have when we are in
          California.

                    JOE
          I think that I got extra energy from
          the crowd tonight. They were CRAzy
          into it!

                    SHELLY
          You are SO going to make it! I just
          know it!!

                    JOE
          I don't know how to explain it, but I
          just KNOW that all of this hard work
          will pay off... The rehearsals, going
          broke to buy band equipment and
          paying for the rehearsal space and
          recording studio time, spending
          weekends putting up show fliers all
          over the city... I promise you that
          we'll have a nice life someday.

                    SHELLY
          We already DO have a nice life, and I
          love every minute that I get to spend
          of it with you.
               (kisses Joe)

The rest of the band jubilantly meanders into the dressing
room, as well as the happy owner of the nightclub.

RANDY, Nightclub owner with pleasant demeanor, wearing a tan
baseball cap with an over-extended brim on it

                    RANDY
          Joe! Joe! Look what you've done! You
          and the band officially SOLD OUT The
          Living Room!
               (Gives Joe a hug)

                    JOE
          Awww, Randy! I'm all sweaty and
          gross!

(CONTINUED)

CONTINUED:

                    RANDY
          I don't care! I'm so proud of you
          kids. Look how all of your hard work
          is paying off...
                    (Hands Joe a stack of
                     $20 bills)

                    JOE
          Thanks Randy, but you know that I do
          this for the love of music - not
          money, right?

                    RANDY
          That's what I love about you. ONE of
          the things that I love about you. It
          is what separates you from the other
          bands that play here.
                    (Turns to Shelly)
          Do you mind if I steal him for a
          minute, Shelly?

                    SHELLY
          Of course not, Randy.

Randy puts his arm around Joe's shoulder and walks him to
the far corner of the brick, graffiti-lined dressing room,
handing Joe an envelope.

                    JOE
          What is this?

                    RANDY
          Just a little dinner money. Once
          Shelly says "Yes", I want you to take
          her to the nicest restaurant that you
          can find in Hollywood and celebrate
          what will be the beginning of a
          beautiful life-long marital
          relationship.

                    JOE
          I can't accept this, Randy. You
          already do a lot for me with all of
          the shows that you've booked The
          Threats onto over the years.

                    RANDY
          Too late. You're holding it and I
          can't take it back.
                    (Walking away)
          You two have fun on the left-coast.
          Great job Threats!

(CONTINUED)

CONTINUED:

Randy exits the dressing room.

                    SHELLY
What was that all about?

                    JOE
           (Trying to buy time
            to make up an excuse
            so as to not spoil
            the engagement
            surprise)
What was what?

                    SHELLY
Randy walking you into the corner and
handing you an envelope.

                    JOE
Oh, he gave me an advance to make
sure that we play the next Providence
show here instead of at The Strand.

                    SHELLY
But you always choose to play here
first, anyway.

                    JOE
Well, maybe he is realizing how The
Threats are now pulling in a crowd
and just wants to make sure we stay
here. Of course I'll continue booking
at The Living Room. This is the best
music venue in New England, and plus,
I love Randy. He's like a father to
me. C'mon, let's say bye to the guys
and get out of here.

                            FADE TO:

EXT. CAR RENTAL LOT IN LOS ANGELES - MID-DAY

Joe is loading suitcases into a convertible car's trunk
before getting in. Shelly is kneeling on passenger seat,
visibly excited, and facing Joe as he loads the trunk.

                    SHELLY
I can't believe that they upgraded
you to a convertible! Now I feel like
a California girl.

Joe gets in the driver's side.

CONTINUED:

                    JOE
          Well, you will be THE prettiest girl
          in all of California this week.

Joe & Shelly drive off.

                    SHELLY
          Do we need to go right to the hotel,
          or can we cruise around for a bit?

                    JOE
          I'll tell you what... Why don't we
          make the most of our first day here.
          I can show you all kinds of things
          and cap it off with an amazing
          Southern California experience and
          surprise. I promise to have us to the
          hotel by midnight, okay?

                    SHELLY
          Sounds awesome to me! Amazing
          California experience & surprise? Any
          hints?

                    JOE
          Sure... You said that you feel like a
          California girl. THAT is your clue
          for the experience. I'm keeping the
          surprise as a surprise.

Driving by Randy's Donuts, which has a huge iconic donut
mounted on the roof.

                    JOE (cont'd)
          How many movies have you seen that
          huge donut in?

                    SHELLY
          Oh my God. That is so cool!

                    JOE
          You haven't seen anything yet...

Joe pulls onto the 405 highway, pointing things out along
the way.

                    JOE (cont'd)
          Downtown L.A. Is way out there to the
          east... See that tall building? It
          was used in the Bruce Willis movie
          'Die Hard'... Way up ahead are the
          Hollywood Hills...
                    (MORE)

CONTINUED:

                    JOE (cont'd)
          You can't see it from here, but the
          Hollywood sign is up in those hills
          toward the right.

                    SHELLY
          Are we close to the beach?

                    JOE
          Absolutely! Let's go see the freaks
          on Venice Beach.

                    SHELLY
          You are so much fun. I love spending
          time with you. I wish we could be
          together every minute of every day.

                    JOE
          You have NO idea how in love with you
          I am. I was going to save this for
          later, but I'll play it for you now.

Joe pulls out a CD from his rocker-style sport-coat.

                    SHELLY
          What is it?

                    JOE
          I borrowed Jeff's 4-track machine and
          recorded a song that I wrote for you.

                    SHELLY
          That is the sweetest thing ever!
          Wait, Jeff actually let you use
          something of his?

                    JOE
          Well, I guess you can say that I
          rented it from him.

                    SHELLY
          I was going to say... considering
          that you write every song for the
          band, and yet he gives you a hard
          time at rehearsals when you just want
          to use his keyboards to show everyone
          a new tune.

                    JOE
          He'll come around... He grew up being
          spoiled because he is the only boy in
          his house, and he never needed to
          share his boy things with his
          sisters.
                    (MORE)

(CONTINUED)

CONTINUED:

> JOE (cont'd)
> Now that we added him to the band, I think he'll learn a lot about teamwork and helping each other along.

> SHELLY
> Umm... YOU are the only boy in YOUR family, with FOUR sisters, and you are the most generous person I know.

> JOE
> Well, maybe the difference is that my Dad eventually didn't live at home and we never had much money. Jeff pretty-much got everything that he ever wanted. His father is quite well-off. I do like Jeff. He'll change. I guess I wonder what I'd be like had my parents stayed together. I'm not sure that I would've been able to play in nightclubs at the age of 14 if Dad was still in the house.

Joe drifts off into thought - maybe thinking of his upbringing.

> SHELLY
> Well? Can I hear the song?

> JOE
> Oh... Yeah... sorry... I hope you like it.

Joe slides the disc into the car's CD player, as they take the "Beach" exit.

<PLAY SONG 'I'D BLEED'>

The song plays while showing cuts of Joe & Shelly holding hands while walking Venice Beach - Stopping to watch chain-saw jugglers and break-dancers - Trying on silly hats from a street vendor and laughing - Walking along the shore, kicking water at each other with pants rolled up and holding their shoes - Eating gelato, sitting at the end of Santa Monica Pier while the sun sets and the song ends.

> SHELLY
> I can't tell you enough how much I LOVE the song that you wrote for me.
> (MORE)

(CONTINUED)

CONTINUED:

SHELLY (cont'd)
It is an entirely different songwriting style than anything that you've written for The Threats. I think that you should do more writing like that.

JOE
Thanks... Do you really think so? It wasn't too boring or too mellow without drums and all?

SHELLY
Are you kidding me? The song made me cry. It allowed me to go right to the words and melody, which I believe is the most powerful aspect of your music.

JOE
Actually, ALL of my songs start out just like what that recording sounds like. Just voice and guitar or piano, and THEN I bring it to the band and discuss my vision of how I want the electric guitar to sound, and make sure that the bass locks-in to what I play for drum parts. Of course, now that we've added Jeff to the band, I've added work to my load by writing all of his parts.

SHELLY
But why doesn't HE come up with parts for the songs?

JOE
Because his Dad bought him some great equipment. Some of the best keyboards out there, but he still needs to learn how to truly play them. LOOK! The sun is about to sink into the water.

SHELLY
I am so in love with you.

JOE
I love you more.

The sun disappears.

JOE (cont'd)
Come-on. I'll prove it to you.

(CONTINUED)

CONTINUED:

Joe leads Shelly by the hand back toward the beginning of the pier.

INT/EXT. DRIVING IN CAR ON MULHOLLAND DRIVE - EARLY EVENING

The car meanders around Mulholland Drive's curves while Joe & Shelly converse.

                    SHELLY
          Wow... What a beautiful drive. I've
          never seen or been on a road like
          this before.

                    JOE
          Wait until you see all of the amazing
          houses that are built up here in the
          daylight. This is where many stars
          live.

                    SHELLY
          I know that you've always talked
          about wanting to live up here. Now
          that I'm here, I can see the
          attraction.

                    JOE
          Yeah... but I'm not a star. Maybe
          someday.

                    SHELLY
          Well you're already a star to me.

Joe pulls the car off to the side of the road, just before the parking lot to the Hollywood Bowl Overlook.

                    JOE
          Awww... That's too bad.

                    SHELLY
          What is wrong?

                    JOE
          The gate is closed... But that's
          alright. This will be worth the
          parking ticket.

                    SHELLY
          I don't get it.

                    JOE
          Come with me.

CONTINUED:

Joe gets out of the car after parking it along the road, and Shelly follows him as he walks around the fence. Both are hanging onto roots and plants so as to not slide down the embankment as they make their way around the fencing to get to the overlook.

                    SHELLY
          Are you crazy?

                    JOE
          Isn't this a fun adventure?

                    SHELLY
          I guess... Although I'm wondering
          what we are doing. Is this the
          surprise you spoke about earlier?

                    JOE
          No, the surprise is later. This is
          the California experience.

                    SHELLY
          I don't get it.

                    JOE
          Hear that music?

                    SHELLY
          I do now. Kind-of sounds like the
          Beach Boys.

The two finally reach the platform that overlooks the Hollywood Bowl, revealing lights radiating from the stage illuminating the sold-out historical venue, which sits down the hill from the overlook.

                    JOE
          Bingo! Take a look! That is the
          Hollywood Bowl. SO many great artists
          have performed there, including The
          Beatles. Tonight, it's The Beach
          Boys. It doesn't get more Southern
          California than this, and we have a
          private balcony seat right here, all
          to ourselves.

Joe sits on the edge of the circular platform, and motions Shelly to do the same. She sits beside him and they begin to kiss. The Beach Boys begin to play the song 'California Dreaming'.

                    SHELLY
          Oh my God, I love this song!

CONTINUED:

                    JOE
          Me too... Actually, here is the
          perfect place to share with you what
          one of my major dreams in life is.

                    SHELLY
          I love when you open up to me about
          your hopes and dreams.

                    JOE
          I've often sat up here and thought
          about this. One of my dreams is to
          have a hit song on the radio, and a
          sold-out show at the Hollywood Bowl.
          The night of the show, I would take a
          helicopter ride from the Valley,
          which would take me over the hills
          directly above this overlook where we
          are sitting so I could see the
          gathering crowd, then have the pilot
          fly me as far out into the horizon as
          we can see right now, at which time I
          would think about the long journey
          that got me to the top. I'd then have
          the pilot turn back and drop me off
          right here, where a car would be
          waiting to take me down the hill to
          perform the concert.

                    SHELLY
          That would be so amazing!

                    JOE
          What is one of your dreams?

                    SHELLY
          My dream is to have your dream come
          true.

                    JOE
          That is a really sweet thing to say,
          but I'm sure that you have dreams of
          your own.

                    SHELLY
          Oh, sure... But none as exciting as
          yours. OK, what is your favorite food
          ever?

CONTINUED:

                    JOE
          Actually, that would be the oven beef
          burrito at my favorite Mexican
          restaurant out here, called Casa
          Vega. It is on Venture Boulevard.
          I'll take you there for a late dinner
          when we leave here. What about yours?

                    SHELLY
          Does it have to be a meal-type of
          food, or does desert count?

                    JOE
          Either, or..

                    SHELLY
          Then chocolate-dipped strawberries...
          or chocolate ice-cream... Actually,
          chocolate anything does it for me.

                    JOE
          I think I knew that. OK... If you
          could go back in time and spend an
          hour with anyone throughout history,
          who would that be?

                    SHELLY
          Hmm... Maybe Marilyn Monroe. She
          seemed to have a glamorous life.

                    JOE
          Is that who you would choose from all
          of history?

                    SHELLY
          Judy Garland?

                    JOE
          It's not like there is a right or
          wrong answer. I was just wondering
          who.

                    SHELLY
          What about you?

                    JOE
          I'd love to have a conversation with
          Jesus Christ, I think it would be
          amazing to look eye-to-eye with him.

                    SHELLY
          That's pretty deep...

(CONTINUED)

CONTINUED:

                    JOE
Who is your favorite family member?

                    SHELLY
Probably my Mom.

                    JOE
And for what reasons?

                    SHELLY
I like the way that she's always
joking around. She makes me laugh.

                    JOE
Any other reason?

                    SHELLY
She takes me shopping? What about
you?

                    JOE
Can I choose someone who has already
passed-away?

                    SHELLY
Sure. Why not?

                    JOE
I'd have to say my Grandfather. He
was a French-Canadian who moved to
the States as a young man, built his
house with his two bare hands, and
was married to my Grandmother for 60
years. I always said that their love
was the truest I've ever witnessed. I
recall that he would raise his beer
at every family function and give a
toast to Grandma, ending it with "and
may I live to be 100, but only if she
is still by my side." They didn't
have the easiest life... Lost a set
of twins at birth, and a daughter to
cancer at age 16.

                    SHELLY
Wow... How does a person recover from
that?

                    JOE
I don't know, but I've never seen
either of them in a bad mood.
                    (MORE)

(CONTINUED)

CONTINUED:

> JOE (cont'd)
> I would spend most of my visits to their house in grandpa's basement wood-shop. He always had scraps of wood for me to build things with, along with my own set of tools. He'd usually let me begin a project, then eventually come down and help me do it the right way. Those are some of my favorite memories ever... The wood-shop, and our annual Boston Red Sox game. He'd take me to see one game per year at Fenway Park. That was magical for me. Before I got into music I wanted to be a professional baseball player, and every year I'd tell my grandfather that I'd be stepping up to that plate one day. Unfortunately, my years of playing in the Little League proved that I didn't have the skills to even come close to thinking about playing in the majors... I miss him a lot.

> SHELLY
> Awww... Those ARE great memories. I'm glad that you and I still go to a Red Sox game at Fenway Park every summer. What would be your saddest memory?

> JOE
> It would definitely be the night that my father left home, and then the months that would follow. There was a definite feeling of abandonment, confusion, and loss. I remember some very awkward and uncomfortable moments where I uncharacteristically lied in effort to pad the feelings of one parent or another. There was the first Christmas morning after the divorce, when Dad came to pick up my sisters and me for a few hours. When I got to his car he handed me a fruit basket, requesting that I give it to Mom. I brought it inside where she insisted that I return it to him, and to tell him that he could keep his damned fruit basket. Instead of doing that, I left it in the garage and told him that Mom said "Thanks, and Merry Christmas"...
> (MORE)

(CONTINUED)

CONTINUED:

> JOE (cont'd)
> There was another time when my mother finally began dating, and when the guy was visiting, my father showed up unexpectedly. I walked up to his car and he asked if I wanted to go out for ice-cream. When I got into his car, he asked who's vehicle was parked at the house. I lied again and told him it was Mom's girlfriend from work. He got out of the car and entered our house. I heard muffled shouting before Dad returned to the car. He said nothing, as my own silence swirled around in my head while I tried to figure out where my eyes should look. The atmosphere in the car became vacuum-like. I will never get divorced - ever. What about you? What was your saddest moment?

> SHELLY
> Honestly?

> JOE
> Of course.

> SHELLY
> It was before we were dating. I was informed that I'd be crowned the homecoming queen at the dance in High School, and Cindy asked you if you'd consider going to the dance with me. I'm not sure, but I think that you told her that you were playing in a nightclub that night. I forget the reason for the rejection, but what I do remember is staying home from the dance and crying all night.

The Beach Boys begin to perform California Girls. Joe stands up and extends a pre-dance hand to Shelly, who takes his hand, stands up and joins Joe in a slow-dance, high above the lights & sounds wafting from the Hollywood Bowl.

> JOE
> I am so sorry, Shelly. I will never give up the chance to dance with you ever again.

Shelly holds Joe even tighter, resting her head on his shoulder. After several seconds of dancing, Joe begins to propose to her.

(CONTINUED)

CONTINUED:

                    JOE (cont'd)
          Do you want to know what my happiest
          moment is?

Shelly pulls her head away from Joe's shoulder, as he
reaches for the engagement ring in his pocket. Joe then gets
down on one knee. Shelly places her shaking hands in front
of her mouth in surprise.

                    JOE (cont'd)
          Shelly, as I look out over the
          horizon here, or across any city, I
          am certain that there is nobody out
          there who is more perfect for me than
          you. Nor, is there any love greater
          in the world than the love that I
          feel for you. And I have no bigger
          dream than the dream I have of
          growing old with you as husband and
          wife. Will you marry me?

Shelly extends her shaking hand so Joe can place the ring on
her ring finger, while wiping away tears with her other
hand.

                    SHELLY
          Yes. Oh my God. Yes! Oh my God!

The two embrace.

                    SHELLY (cont'd)
          You just made my dream come true. I
          never wanted to tell you because I
          didn't want you to feel pressured. I
          am so happy. I love you so much.

                              DISSOLVE TO:

INT. CASA VEGA MEXICAN RESTAURANT - LATER IN THE EVENING

Joe and Shelly are sitting at their table as Joe takes care
of the check while they converse.

                    SHELLY
          You were right. That WAS a great
          burrito.

                    JOE
          I told you...

                                        (CONTINUED)

CONTINUED:

                         SHELLY
          OK, I'll add that to my list of
          favorite foods, but after chocolate.

                         JOE
          Maybe it's all of that chocolate that
          makes you so sweet.

                         SHELLY
          What is it about me that makes you
          want to marry me instead of anybody
          else in the world?

                         JOE
          Seriously? It is EVERYTHING about
          you... The way you smile and laugh,
          talk, kiss... The way that we can
          completely be ourselves when we are
          with each other... How I long for you
          when we are miles apart, or even on
          opposite sides of the same crowded
          room... I love the way that your hand
          always seems to be reaching out for
          mine at the very same time I go to
          reach for yours... I like the way
          that we both have faith in God. If
          there is such a thing as soul-mates,
          it MUST be you for me. The bonus is
          that you are always the prettiest
          girl in whatever place we are at, and
          I can't take my eyes off of you, even
          after all of these years of dating.
          I'm sure that every other guy has a
          tough time keeping their eyes off of
          you, too.

                         SHELLY
          I love you so much... but I'm hardly
          ever the most pretty girl in the
          room.

                         JOE
          Are you kidding me? OK, I'll prove
          it.

                         SHELLY
          What? I don't think that is something
          that can be proven.

Joe fakes a really big yawn, then gazes around the room.
Everyone is going about their conversations and meals as
they were prior to Joe's yawn. Shelly notices Joe looking
around the room, wondering what he is looking for.

(CONTINUED)

CONTINUED:

Eventually, She can't help but to yawn, too, after seeing
Joe's dramatic yawn, and they both look around to see most
guys in the room beginning to yawn, and we begin to hear
loud yawning noises from all corners of the restaurant.

                    JOE
          I rest my case. Let's get out of
          here, my pretty fiance.

                    SHELLY
          "Fiance". I like hearing that.

As Joe and Shelly exit the restaurant, several male heads
turn to watch Shelly pass by, while they continue to yawn.

EXT. OUTSIDE MEXICAN RESTAURANT AT VALET STAND - MOMENTS
LATER

Joe and Shelly wait for the rental car to be brought to them
when a fancy sports car pulls up.

                    SHELLY
          Wow. Look at that car.

The driver gets out, looking surprised and excited.

LENNY, Slick-looking Record Producer

                    LENNY
          Joe! Wow! What are you doing in L.A.?

Shelly turns to Joe.

                    SHELLY
          You know him?

                    JOE
          Holy crap! When did you get this car,
          Lenny?

                    LENNY
          I picked it up about a month ago.
          Record sales have been great. It's
          amazing bumping into you like this.
          What brings you out here this time?

                    JOE
          Well, you know me... I've got a
          suitcase full of my music that I'm
          hoping to get into the right hands at
          the record labels this week.

                                              (CONTINUED)

CONTINUED:

Shelly clears her throat.

                    JOE (cont'd)
          Oh... and I've got some big news.
          Shelly and I just got engaged
          tonight. I can't believe that you two
          haven't met yet. Shelly, this is
          Lenny - Lenny, Shelly.

                    LENNY
          Well, I've certainly heard lots of
          flattering things about you over the
          years. Nice to finally meet you, and
          congratulations to both of you. Wow!

                    SHELLY
          Thank you, and nice meeting you, too,
          Lenny.

                    LENNY
          Why don't you both join me inside and
          I'll buy a round of drinks to
          celebrate your engagement?

                    JOE
          That's very generous of you, Lenny,
          but we are on the verge of falling
          asleep on our feet, considering the
          jet-lag. We just got in this morning
          and haven't stopped, so we're going
          to head to our hotel. What about one
          night this week?

                    LENNY
          Awww, that's too bad. I'm leaving for
          Phoenix tomorrow afternoon and won't
          be back until next week. Where are
          you staying?

                    JOE
          Where I always stay out here, The
          Sportsman's Lodge on Ventura and
          Coldwater. I'm not sure if we will
          spend our entire week there, though,
          as the prices have almost doubled
          since I was here just half a year
          ago.

                    LENNY
          I'll bet... It has become quite
          trendy. You'll see tour buses from
          famous bands there almost every
          night.
                    (MORE)

                                        (CONTINUED)

CONTINUED:

                    LENNY (cont'd)
          It is where they stay when in Los
          Angeles. I'll tell you what, my cat
          sitter canceled on me and I haven't
          found a replacement as of yet. Why
          don't you two love-birds stay at my
          condo this week? All I ask is that
          you feed "Yaz" and the place is
          yours, free of charge.

                    JOE
          Are you kidding? That would be
          awesome!

                    LENNY
          It's a win-win for all of us. Call me
          in the morning and I'll give you the
          address. I'm in a new pad. The key
          will be under the mat, and I'll leave
          a note with instructions for Yaz on
          the table. You two may just decide on
          moving out here once you settle into
          the California life for a week. I'd
          lend you my old car, but it isn't
          registered currently. If you do
          decide to move here someday, I'll
          GIVE you that car. You know that this
          is the place to be to advance your
          music career, Joe.

                    JOE
          Yeah, I know... Man, you are the
          best, Lenny. Thank you so much. Don't
          worry about Yaz while you are away,
          we'll take great care of him. Shelly
          is a big cat person, and has two of
          her own.

The valet pulls up with Joe's rental car. Joe & Shelly hug
Lenny, get into the car and pull away.

                                        FADE TO:

INT. LENNY'S APARTMENT - EARLY MORNING

Joe carries in the last of the suitcases while Shelly
marvels at all of the music memorabilia/trophies that Lenny
has hanging on the walls.

                    JOE
          Cool condo, huh?

                                        (CONTINUED)

CONTINUED:

                          SHELLY
              I'll say... Wow, it looks like Lenny
              is a really accomplished producer.
              Look at all of these gold records,
              Billboard Magazine reviews, photos...

                          JOE
              Yeah, Lenny has done a lot.

                          SHELLY
              You seem to know him pretty well. Has
              he done anything for you in the music
              industry?

                          JOE
              I went through grade school with
              Lenny's youngest brother, Stan. Their
              family was originally from our
              hometown of Cumberland... So no,
              Lenny hasn't pro-actively helped me
              in the industry yet.

                          SHELLY
              Why not?

                          JOE
              A prophet is without honor only in
              his hometown, among his relatives,
              and in his own home.

                          SHELLY
              Huh?

                          JOE
              That is something which was stated by
              Jesus in The Bible. Not that I am
              comparing myself to a prophet at all,
              but I think that the concept is
              relevant, or at least how I perceive
              it to be...

                          SHELLY
              I'm still not following.

                          JOE
              Well, this saying could be taken a
              few different ways. One of the ways
              could be that when you grow up with,
              and/or live with someone, they are a
              familiar person, which makes them a
              most "normal" person, rather than
              someone that is deemed "special or
              extraordinary".
                          (MORE)

CONTINUED:

> JOE (cont'd)
> For instance, relatives and friends
> of The Beatles viewed them very
> differently than the rest of the
> world. They were "just normal people"
> to those that they grew up with, but
> to the rest of the world they were
> icons and idols. I think in the case
> of Lenny, he's been recording with
> folks that we grew up listening to on
> the radio as kids, which is much more
> exciting to him, I'd imagine, than
> recording someone that lived two
> streets over and may have written
> some descent songs. Plus, he
> concentrates on making records with
> big sports celebrities. It is his
> niche.

> SHELLY
> I guess that I hear what you are
> saying. It is too bad, though. I'm
> sure that he has a lot of connections
> that could really do something for
> you.

> JOE
> He does, and that is why I don't push
> Lenny to take me on as a project.
> When I am hanging out with him, often
> times I am meeting some of those
> connections. I feel that things will
> happen in due time. I don't want to
> be pushy, or make it appear that I am
> friends with anyone because of what
> they might be able to do for me, you
> know? Lenny is a good friend of mine.
> I've liked and respected him long
> before he was in any position to help
> with my musical career.

> SHELLY
> Yes, I can see your point, but I'm
> sure that it can be frustrating.

> JOE
> Of course it can be... I just keep
> telling myself that MY time will
> come, eventually. The important thing
> is to just keep on playing, writing,
> and being true to myself and the
> craft of making music.

(CONTINUED)

CONTINUED:

A meow is heard from the loft above, and Yaz the cat comes running down the stairs.

                    JOE (cont'd)
          There's Yaz!

Joe leans over and picks up the cat, showing it to Shelly.

                    JOE (cont'd)
          This guy must be approaching 20 years
          old. Lenny has had him forever.

                    SHELLY
          He looks like he is in great shape.
          Seems very alert and playful.

                    JOE
          This cat is SO smart. Do you know
          that Yaz has predicted every
          earthquake that has happened since
          Lenny has lived in L.A.?

                    SHELLY
          What? How?

                    JOE
          Lenny says that Yaz will begin to
          freak out and run around the
          apartment as fast as he can, leaping
          from one piece of furniture to
          another. Within 2 minutes of that
          behavior, an earthquake happens, each
          and every time.

                    SHELLY
          Oooo... That is scary. I don't think
          I'll ever want to live here.

                    JOE
          Well, back home we get hurricanes and
          blizzards, so I think there is risk
          no matter where you live.

                    SHELLY
          I'll take the blizzards, thank you.

                    JOE
          Come on... I want to introduce my
          fiance to some of my L.A. Friends.

                                        FADE TO:

EXT. SECURITY GATE AT SUNSET-GOWER STUDIOS - LATE MORNING

Joe pulls up to the security gate and rolls down the window.
Security guard walks over.

CARLOS, Uniformed security guard

                    CARLOS
          Joe! Long time! Whassup my man?

                    JOE
          Carlos, my friend! Yeah, it's been a
          few months. What's going on?

                    CARLOS
          You know... Hardly working. Catching
          a tan in the California sun, baby.
          Who's the lady?

                    JOE
          This is Shelly, who happens to be my
          fiance as of last night!

                    CARLOS
          WHAAAAAT?? Man, congratulations! Nice
          to meet you.

                    SHELLY
          Nice to meet you, too.

                    CARLOS
          Now how did YOU get to land such a
          pretty girl as Shelly?

                    JOE
          Ha Ha... Screw you, Carlos!

                    CARLOS
          You know I'm just messin' wicha dude.
          Heading to Married with Children?

                    JOE
          Yeah, we've got a diamond ring to
          show around. Don't call ahead to the
          studio. I want to surprise Steven.

                    CARLOS
          You got it. Here's your pass. You
          know the drill... Great seeing you,
          Bro.

                    JOE
          I'll see you again. Thanks Carlos.

CONTINUED:

CUT TO:

INT. STUDIO SET OF MARRIED W/CHILDREN - MOMENTS LATER

Joe and Shelly walk past the buffet table. Joe grabs 2
waters from it as they continue to walk along the side of
the empty audience bleachers. There is a rehearsal with the
actors happening on the set. Joe hands the waters to Shelly,
and sneaks up on one of the stage-hands from behind and
covers his eyes.

BART, Stage Hand. Holding a clipboard.

                    BART
          What the...?

Joe uncovers Bart's eyes

                    BART (cont'd)
               (in an excited, but
                quiet voice)
          Joe! What a great surprise. What are
          you doing out here this week?

                    JOE
          Hey Bart... I'm shopping my music
          around to some record labels, and
          this...

Joe lifts Shelly's hand, pointing out her ring finger.

                    BART
          Congratulations! You must be Shelly.
          I'm Bart.

                    SHELLY
          Nice to meet you, Bart, and thank
          you.

                    BART
          Does Steven know yet?

                    JOE
          Not yet. He doesn't even know that
          I'm in town. How are rehearsals
          going?

                    BART
          They'll be breaking for lunch soon.
          Buck has a big role in this scene, so
          Steven is laser-focused on getting
          him to do a major trick right now.
                    (MORE)

(CONTINUED)

CONTINUED:
                          BART (cont'd)
          Come-on, I'll take you to Steven and
          Buck's dressing room. He'll be more
          surprised if he doesn't see you out
          here.

                          JOE
          Actually, we'll just linger here for
          a few and watch the rest of the
          rehearsal, if that's cool with you.
          Shelly has never been on a real
          studio set before, and she loves the
          show.

                          BART
          By all means... You know where
          everything is, Joe. Make yourself at
          home. I need to run something to the
          control room, but let's catch up
          later. Great seeing you, and nice to
          meet you, Shelly. I'm happy for you
          two!

                          JOE
          Thanks, man.

                          SHELLY
          This is SO cool... I can't believe I
          am watching a Married w/ Children
          rehearsal in real life.

                          JOE
          I'm glad that you are having fun. I
          love sharing experiences like this
          with you.

The rehearsal appears to be winding down.

                          JOE (cont'd)
          Let's head to Steven's dressing room.

                                        CUT TO:

INT. STEVEN'S AND BUCK-THE-DOG'S DRESSING ROOM - MOMENTS
LATER

Joe fills Buck-the Dog's water dish with the water bottles
he grabbed from the buffet table, then sits on a love-seat
while Shelly primps her hair in the dressing room mirror.
The door opens and Buck excitingly leaps over to Joe. Steven
walks in and is very surprised.

                                        (CONTINUED)

CONTINUED:

                    JOE
          Buck! There's my boy!

Joe nestles his head against Buck's head while petting his
back. Buck begins to lick Joe's face.

STEVEN, Hollywood Animal Trainer, and owner of Buck the Dog

                    STEVEN
          Joe! What a surprise! I first saw
          this beautiful woman in front of my
          mirror and thought that it must be my
          lucky day, and then I turn and see
          you! Wow!

Joe gets up and the two hug.

                    JOE
          I've got some news, brother... I'd
          like you to meet Shelly, who is now
          my fiance.

                    STEVEN
          Are you kidding me? That's wonderful!
          Congratulations!

Steven gives Shelly a hug.

                    SHELLY
          Thank you, Steven.

                    STEVEN
          It took an engagement for me to
          finally meet you after all these
          years of Joe coming out here. You are
          even prettier than Joe had described.

                    SHELLY
          Awww...

                    STEVEN
          I'm sure that you already know this,
          or else you wouldn't have said "yes",
          but you've got yourself a great guy
          there. Joe's one of my best friends
          on the planet, and there is a reason
          for that. He is genuine.

                    SHELLY
          Yeah... I'm very lucky. He's one in a
          million... a billion, actually.

(CONTINUED)

CONTINUED:

                    JOE
          That's enough... I'm the lucky one to
          have both of you in my life. How has
          the show been going?

                    STEVEN
          Stressful as always. Everyone thinks
          that I should be able to snap my
          fingers and have Buck walk across the
          room on his hind legs, lock the front
          door, then open the fridge and grab a
          steak in one shot without any
          cutaways.

                    JOE
          Well, why would this week's show be
          different than any other show? Ha
          Ha... You've always been under that
          kind of pressure. It's because you
          deliver, so they expect those
          miracles every time. It is called
          being the best at what you do.

                    STEVEN
          Yeah, well if it gave me a rest every
          now and then, I wouldn't mind being
          mediocre. I am tired.

                    JOE
          OK... I didn't actually hear you say
          that.

                    STEVEN
          So what are your plans while you are
          out here?

                    JOE
          Mostly trying to get some of my music
          in the hands of record company execs,
          and showing Shelly around Los
          Angeles.

                    STEVEN
          Why don't you come out to my ranch
          this weekend? I could show Shelly the
          animals.

                    SHELLY
          That would be really neat!

                                    (CONTINUED)

CONTINUED:

                         JOE
          It would be, but Steven's ranch is an
          hour and a half away from here and
          our flight leaves in the afternoon on
          Saturday. We will definitely need to
          factor that in for the next time
          we're out here.

                         STEVEN
          When are you guys just going to move
          out here? Joe, you are here all the
          time anyway, and I can probably get
          you a job on the studio lot.

                         JOE
          Thanks, Bro, but we'll need to cross
          that bridge when we get to it.
          Anyway, I'm going to let you get to
          lunch, and I'm going to try and get
          some record label interest for my
          music.

                         STEVEN
          Not before walking Buck for me.

                         JOE
          I was hoping you'd say that. Come-on
          Buck!

Joe grabs the leash that hangs near the door, and he and
Buck exit the room.

                                        CUT TO:

INT./EXT. INSIDE CAR AT THE CURB OUTSIDE CAPITOL RECORDS -
AFTERNOON

Joe grabs 4 padded envelopes from a bag on the back seat and
hands one to Shelly, along with a list of names and a black
sharpie marker.

                         JOE
          Shelly, would you mind finding the
          person's name under Capitol Records
          and writing it on the envelope? Your
          handwriting is much better than mine.

                         SHELLY
          Sure. What is in it?

CONTINUED:

                    JOE
          A demo recording of The Threats and
          our bio.

                    SHELLY
          There is only one name under each
          record company on this list. Why are
          you bringing in four packages?

                    JOE
          I got those names from Rick, the
          Program Director at the radio station
          back home. Those are promotional
          people for the labels. They don't
          actually sign bands, but their names
          will get me past the security guards.
          Rick said that I can use him as a
          reference. They all need Rick to play
          their label's artists on the radio in
          New England so they won't deny me
          access. The people who actually do
          the signing are in the A&R
          department, which I will find once I
          am in there...

                    SHELLY
          A&R?

                    JOE
          A&R stands for Artists & Repertoire.
          They are THE most important people in
          any record company to someone that is
          looking for a record deal because
          they are who actually signs the
          artists to the label. Wish me luck!

Shelly hands Joe the envelope and leans over to give him a
kiss.

                    SHELLY
          Go get 'em, my talented fiance!

INT. CAPITOL RECORDS LOBBY - MOMENTS LATER

Joe enters the round Capitol Records building, where he is
greeted by a security guard behind a desk.

                    SECURITY GUARD
          May I help you?

CONTINUED:

                    JOE
          Good afternoon. I am here to see Rob
          Rounder.

The security guard picks up a phone.

                    SECURITY GUARD
          And may I announce to him who's
          visiting?

                    JOE
          Of course. I'm Joe Silva, on behalf
          of Rick McKay from WAAF Radio.

                    SECURITY GUARD
               (Muffled speaking
                into phone receiver)
          OK, please write your name on this
          badge and stick it onto your jacket
          for me. Rob's office is 516. The
          elevators are just off to the right
          there.

                    JOE
          Oh... OK, Thank you. I thought that
          the 5th floor was A&R for some
          reason.

                    SECURITY GUARD
          No, A&R has always been on the 9th
          floor.

                    JOE
          Thanks for your help.

                                        CUT TO:

INT. INSIDE ELEVATOR - MOMENTS LATER

Joe goes to hit the 5th floor button, then looks at the
stack of promotional packages in his hands and realizes that
he should get rid of the "extra" packages before visiting
with Rob. He presses the 9th floor button instead, letting
out a breath of nervousness. The door opens to a hallway
full of offices. Joe walks into the first two unoccupied
offices that he passes and leaves a package on each desk. As
he is about to enter the third, he realizes that there is a
record executive sitting at the desk, speaking on the phone.
He leans in and places a package on his desk.

RECORD EXECUTIVE, Wearing a suit and smoking a cigar

                                        (CONTINUED)

CONTINUED:

                      RECORD EXECUTIVE
                (Into the phone)
      Um, hold on a minute Clive...
                (Shouting out to Joe,
                 who is already down
                 the hall and almost
                 in the elevator)
      Hey! Who are you? How did you get up
      here?

Back in the elevator, Joe breathes a sigh of relief and hits
the 5th floor button.

                                  CUT TO:

INT. ROB ROUNDER'S OFFICE - MOMENTS LATER

Joe sits in an over-sized chair and feels small, as Rob and
Joe converse.

ROB ROUNDER, Capitol Records Radio Promotion Manager

                      ROB ROUNDER
      So, you're friends with Rick, huh?

                          JOE
      Yes, I've known Rick a long time. I
      went to school with his younger
      brother.

                      ROB ROUNDER
      Oh, so you aren't in the radio
      business yourself?

                          JOE
      Well, my band gets PLAYED on the
      radio on Sunday nights, but I am
      hoping for more airplay someday,
      which is why I'm here. Would you be
      willing to give my music a listening
      to, and if you like it, pass it along
      to some of the A&R people here?

                      ROB ROUNDER
      No promises, but I'll see what I can
      do. Unsolicited material doesn't
      usually get listened to.

                          JOE
      Unsolicited?

Rob looks at his watch.

                              (CONTINUED)

CONTINUED:

                    ROB ROUNDER
          Well, I've got another meeting.
          Please tell Rick that I said hello
          when you see him.

Rob walks Joe out the door.

                    JOE
          I will. Thanks. I hope that you'll
          listen to my music. I think you'd
          really like my band.

                                        CUT TO:

EXT. GETTING BACK INTO CAR - MOMENTS LATER

Joe jumps into the car and immediately starts it up and
pulls away.

                    SHELLY
          So? How did it go?

                    JOE
          Well, time will tell. Hopefully they
          will like the tunes.

                    SHELLY
          Where are we off to now?

                    JOE
          I'm thinking we should hit a few more
          record labels

<RECOMMENDED SONG 'CALIFORNIA SUN' BY THE RAMONES>

Here, we see lots of quick cuts of Joe driving, running in
and out of various record company buildings with his
packages, speaking with security guards, getting into
elevators, darting down halls after leaving promotional
packages in various offices. We also see cuts to Shelly,
somewhat bored, leaning her head out of the car at one stop,
trying to get some California sun, then outside leaning on
the car at another stop, and eventually laying on the hood
at yet another stop.

                                        FADE TO:

EXT. SWIMMING POOL AT LENNY'S CONDO COMPLEX - EARLY
AFTERNOON

Shelly swims over to Joe, who is sitting on the rim of the
pool with a rock-style long sleeve shirt on and his jeans
rolled up, while his legs wade in the water. Joe has a stack
of trade magazines that he is combing through.

                    SHELLY
          Aren't you going to come in the
          water? It's our last full day here.

                    JOE
          I know. Last full day, so I want to
          make sure that I've hit every
          opportunity that I can while we are
          out here.

                    SHELLY
          But you've gone to just about every
          record company out here already.

                    JOE
          Yeah, but I'm realizing that we
          didn't stop at Warner Brothers, and I
          just got the name of a new A&R person
          there out of this Hollywood Reporter
          magazine. I'm just going to make a
          quick run over there.

                    SHELLY
          Really? Now?

                    JOE
          You don't have to come. You can stay
          in the pool. They are just in
          Burbank, so I'll be back in like
          forty minutes, OK?

                    SHELLY
          It's not that. It's just that it
          would be nice to spend some romantic
          fiance time together in the sun
          before we leave.

                    JOE
          I promise that we will, right when I
          get back.

Joe gives Shelly a kiss and gets up from the side of the
pool and starts walking away.

(CONTINUED)

CONTINUED:

> JOE (cont'd)
> We will have a much better life if I
> can land a record deal.

> FADE TO:

INT. THE THREATS REHEARSAL SPACE - EVENING

Band members are assembling, tuning, etc., Joe's friend and
roadie, Donny, is helping to stack one amplifier on top of
another one. A few of the band member's girlfriends are
sitting on the couch sipping wine coolers. Joe walks into
the room and Shelly follows.

> JOE
> WOO-HOO!!

Everyone stops what they are doing and looks over at Joe.

> JOE (cont'd)
> I just got off the phone with Randy
> at the Living Room. We are opening
> for Joan Jett in a few weeks! I LOVE
> Rock & Roll!!

Everyone begins to cheer, celebrate.

DONNY, Muscular guy in his early twenties

> DONNY
> Well?? You just got back from L.A.,
> do you have more news?

> JOE
> L.A. Was great! I made it into a
> bunch of record companies and dropped
> off our music, so fingers crossed on
> The Threats getting discovered!

More celebration by the band members.

> DONNY
> Seriously? Is that it?

Donny secretly motions to Joe, pointing at his ring finger.

> JOE
> Of course not! I save the best news
> for last. I'd like to introduce you
> to the future Mrs. Silva!

(CONTINUED)

CONTINUED:

Everyone gathers around Shelly, giving hugs and gushing
about her engagement ring.

JEFF, Keyboardist of the band. A bit more stiff and dressed
a little preppy vs. The rock style of the other band
members.

                    JEFF
          So when is the big day going to be?

                    SHELLY
          Well, we haven't quite set a date
          yet.

GIRLFRIEND #1, Dressed provocatively, chewing a wad of gum.

                    GIRLFRIEND #1
          WHAT? Girl, you need to set a date
          for ring number two to be added to
          that finger.

                    SHELLY
          We will figure it out, eventually.
          Joe wants to get closer to a record
          deal before we say "I Do".

                    JEFF
          Considering this industry, Joe might
          hit the lottery sooner.

                    JOE
          No kidding... How long is a
          millennium?

The guys go back about their business in getting ready to
rehearse. A minute or so goes by and we see Shelly
noticeably upset, leaving the room. Joe doesn't notice as he
settles-in behind his drum set. Girlfriend #2 (who is
dressed more classy than Girlfriend #1) walks out to look
after Shelly.

                                        FADE TO:

INT. POST OFFICE - EARLY AFTERNOON (THREE WEEKS LATER)

Joe walks up to the clerk who is behind the counter, handing
him a slip.

                    JOE
          Hi. This was in my PO Box. It says
          that I received a package that is too
          large for my box?

                                        (CONTINUED)

CONTINUED:

POST OFFICE CLERK, Skinny guy wearing Post Office uniform.
Late forties, with a mustache

                    POST OFFICE CLERK
          Hey Joe! Yes, you have LOTS of
          packages that are too big. I remember
          seeing them. They are all from
          California. I'll get them in a
          minute. First, would you mind signing
          the story that was in the newspaper
          about the food drive benefit show
          that you played a month or so back?

                    JOE
          You kept a copy of that? Of course
          I'll sign it.

                    POST OFFICE CLERK
          Yes, I actually kept two copies. Let
          me go get them from my locker. You
          can have one of them.

The clerk leaves his post, and Joe turns around to see a
line of people that also have Post Office business to do. A
minute passes while the clerk is away and several folks in
line are getting restless. Some even turn around in a huff
and leave. Finally, the unapologetic clerk returns, handing
Joe two newspapers and a sharpie.

                    POST OFFICE CLERK (cont'd)
          If you could write one copy out to
          Kevin, that'd be great. The other one
          is yours.

                    JOE
          No problem... and thanks for the
          extra copy. I'll save it for when I
          have kids someday and can give it to
          them.

                    POST OFFICE CLERK
          Actually, could you write it out to
          "My dear friend Kevin"? My girlfriend
          would get a kick out of that.

Joe hears more heavy sighs and breathing from the folks
waiting in line.

                    JOE
          I'm sorry, I already wrote "To
          Kevin". I really need to get to a
          sound-check. Would you mind finding
          my packages, please?

(CONTINUED)

CONTINUED:

                    POST OFFICE CLERK
          Yes... Of course. I heard on the
          radio that you guys are playing with
          Joan Jett tonight. Hey, you don't
          have any complimentary tickets for
          tonight's show on you, do ya?

                    JOE
          I'm sorry, Kevin. I don't. But I
          really do need to get out of here.

                    POST OFFICE CLERK
          Right away...

The clerk walks away again, and Joe turns to apologize to
the folks waiting in line. He gets recognized by a former
classmate from high-school, who is also a cousin of Shelly's
friend Cindy.

KAREN, Red-headed girl, nasally voice

                    KAREN
          Joe! Oh my God, I'm going to your
          concert tonight!

Joe can't quite remember her name.

                    JOE
          Hey you! It's been forever. Cool that
          you got a ticket for the show.

                    KAREN
          Yeah, as soon as my cousin told me a
          few weeks ago that she would be going
          with Shelly and some other friends I
          drove downtown and picked up a pair
          myself. Did I hear that you and
          Shelly are going to England or
          something?

                    JOE
          England? Maybe someday.

The post office clerk returns with a box full of packages.

                    JOE (cont'd)
          Wow... Those are all mine?

                    POST OFFICE CLERK
          All yours, my friend. Looks like
          you've got some activity in Los
          Angeles... Capitol Records, A&M
          Records, Warner Brothers...

                                        (CONTINUED)

CONTINUED:

                    JOE
          OK, Thanks!

Joe picks up the box of packages with a look of excitement
on his face and begins to hurry into the PO Box room so he
can open the packages on the table in there.

                    POST OFFICE CLERK
          Have a great show tonight, Joe!

                    KAREN
          Yeah, break a leg, Joe! I'll be in
          the crowd cheering!

                    JOE
          Thanks everyone!

                                        CUT TO:

INT. PO BOX ROOM IN POST OFFICE - MOMENTS LATER

Joe opens package after package, only to find all of his
promotional packages returned to him from the record
companies. Each company included a form letter explaining
that the material was not listened to and returned because
it was unsolicited (not presented to the record labels by a
known entertainment lawyer or reputable manager). The
excitement in Joe's face is replaced by anger and
disappointment. He walks over to the pay phone and calls
Shelly.

                    SHELLY
               (off screen)
          Hello?

                    JOE
               (tone of
                disappointment)
          Hi Babe, it's me.

                    SHELLY
               (off screen)
          What's the matter? You don't sound
          like yourself. Did tonight's show get
          canceled?

                    JOE
          No. Worse... You know all of those
          promo-packages that I dropped off at
          the record companies?

                                        (CONTINUED)

CONTINUED:

                    SHELLY
               (off screen)
     Well, Yeah, that was sort-of most of
     our trip to Los Angeles.

                    JOE
     Yeah, well, I'm sort-of looking at
     every single one of them right now.

                    SHELLY
               (off screen)
     What are you talking about?

                    JOE
               (speaking too loudly
                for being in a
                public place)
     I'm talking about every freaking one
     of them being returned to me. I'm at
     the post office right now. Not one
     freaking company listened to any of
     the songs!

                    SHELLY
               (off screen)
     Really? Why?

Karen pokes her head into the PO Box room.

                    KAREN
     Everything OK in here?

                    JOE
     Yes. Everything is fine. I'm talking
     to Shelly.

Karen gives a look of disapproval and leaves the post
office.

                    SHELLY
               (off screen)
     What?

                    JOE
     No... Cindy's cousin is here at the
     post office. She just asked me a
     question.

                    SHELLY
               (off screen)
     Oh, Karen?

CONTINUED:

                    JOE
          Yeah, I think that's her name.

                    SHELLY
               (off screen)
          Cool. Cindy and I might meet up with
          her at the show tonight. I'm just
          going to drive up there with Cindy.
          Can you put us on the guest list?

                    JOE
          Sure... But don't you want to come to
          sound-check with us and meet Joan
          Jett?

                    SHELLY
               (off screen)
          I guess I'll pass on sound-check, but
          I look forward to your show. Say
          hello to her for me (laughs).

                    JOE
          Whatever.

                    SHELLY
               (off screen)
          Are you upset?

                    JOE
          Nope. I'll just see you at the show.
          Do you want to hear about these
          returned packages?

                    SHELLY
               (off screen)
          Oh... I would, but Cindy is pulling
          up right now. Can you tell me later?

                    JOE
          She's picking you up now? It is still
          afternoon.

                    SHELLY
          Yeah, but we are going to go
          cruising. Maybe catch a bite
          somewhere. OK, let me let you go.
          Love ya!

                    JOE
          Love y...

Joe notices that Shelly hung up the phone before he could
respond.

CONTINUED:

He slams the phone while hanging it up, then notices that Karen is sitting in her car and watching him through the window. He begins to gather all of the promotional packages that are piled on the table while shaking his head.

                                        FADE TO:

EXT. LOAD-IN DOOR AT THE LIVING ROOM - EARLY EVENING

The band is unloading their gear from a van into the music venue for their performance later in the evening, opening for Joan Jett. Donny, as usual, is carrying the largest/ heaviest gear. Joe is hauling a bass drum.

                    JOE
          Dude! You're going to break your
          back. Put that amp down and I'll give
          you a hand after I get this bass drum
          inside.

                    DONNY
               (grunting)
          Aghh!! I've got this. You need to
          save your energy for the show.

They both walk inside with their load of equipment.

                                        CUT TO:

INT. THE LIVING ROOM MAIN CONCERT ROOM - MOMENTS LATER

Joe is pre-setting up his drums in the middle of the room while Joan Jett's band sets up for their sound-check on the stage. Donny is leaning over the large amp that he carried, catching his breath.

                    JOE
          Donny, I don't know what we'd do
          without you over the years. I wish we
          could actually pay you for all the
          work that you do, but I'll make sure
          you get some extra beer tonight.

                    DONNY
          Are you kidding me? The experiences
          that you give me are priceless.
               (MORE)

                                        (CONTINUED)

CONTINUED:

>   DONNY (cont'd)
> Look, there's Joan Jett sound-
> checking, then I get to see her show
> for free after yours, and I'm sure
> that we'll be hanging out with her
> later tonight like all the other big
> bands that you guys open for. Who
> else is doing this??

>   JOE
> That's true... and funny how that's
> become our motto over the years. Who
> else IS doing this??

Keebler the stage manager walks over.

>   JOE (cont'd)
> Hey Keebler.

>   KEEBLER
> Big night tonight. Going to be over
> packed. When your set is over, just
> push your amps toward the back of the
> stage along the wall where the stage
> door is. You guys are here for the
> duration. We won't be able to move
> anything out of the building until
> the show is over and the crowd is
> gone.

>   JOE
> Donny did you hear that? Amps to the
> back of the stage after our show.
> Don't pull anything off until the end
> of the night.

Donny, still leaning on the amp, signals to Joe that he
heard, while watching Joan get set-up on the stage.

>   KEEBLER
> Where is your sexy shadow?

>   JOE
> Shelly?

>   KEEBLER
> Yes. I don't think I recall her ever
> missing a sound-check. Is she sick?

>   JOE
> Nah, she'll be here later. Coming
> with her friend tonight.

CONTINUED:

> KEEBLER
> Well, I hope she gets here early
> enough to actually see you on the
> stage. The show has been sold out for
> weeks and people have been lining up
> at the front door since this morning
> to get a good spot.

Keebler walks away, and Donny walks over to Joe while he
adjusts the drums.

> DONNY
> Everything alright between you and
> Shelly?

> JOE
> Yeah... Why do you ask?

> DONNY
> I don't know. It just seemed like
> there was a weird vibe with her over
> the past few rehearsals... and it's
> true that she never misses a sound-
> check.

> JOE
> I think that Shelly just feels bad
> for Cindy, now that she is engaged
> and Cindy still has no boyfriend.
> That's probably why she decided to
> come with her tonight instead of with
> us.

The rest of The Threats are milling around the room,
checking out their equipment before it goes onto the stage.
Joan Jett breaks into 'I Love Rock & Roll' for a sound-check
song.

<SUGGESTED LISTENING 'I LOVE ROCK & ROLL' BY JOAN JETT>

> FADE TO:

INT. DRESSING ROOM - LATER THAT EVENING

The band members are visible excited about getting onto the
stage soon. Joe is in the corner saying his ritual pre-show
prayer, by himself. Donny walks into the dressing room.

> DONNY
> Man, I don't think I've EVER seen
> this place so packed.
> (MORE)

> (CONTINUED)

CONTINUED:

                    DONNY (cont'd)
          You guys are going to kick-butt
          tonight! There's water on the stage
          for each of you.

Donny notices Joe in the corner and walks toward him.
Keebler enters the dressing room, wielding his flashlight.

                    KEEBLER
          Alright, Threats - Time to rock the
          house!

Donny hands Joe a towel to bring to the stage.

                    DONNY
          Are you nervous tonight?

                    JOE
          Not about the show.

                    DONNY
          I placed two beers behind your drums
          as you requested. It took me forever
          to get them from the bar. It is SO
          packed tonight.

                    JOE
          Thanks, man. Did you happen to see
          Shelly out there?

                    DONNY
          Yeah, she's standing along the side
          wall... but just concentrate on your
          concert.

Joe and Donny head toward the dressing room door to catch up
with Keebler and the rest of the band on the way to the
stage.

                    JOE
          What's that supposed to mean?

                    DONNY
          Dude, this is another big show for
          you. Just do what you do best and
          don't let anything else distract you.

                    JOE
          Why are you talking like that? I've
          played a gazillion shows.

                    DONNY
          Who else is doing this?

CONTINUED:

Donny pats Joe's back, pushing him out of the dressing room.

                                        CUT TO:

INT. ON STAGE - ABOUT 45 MINUTES INTO THE THREATS' CONCERT

<PLAY SONG 'MY TODAY MY TOMORROW'>

Joe is extremely sweaty from his performance as the lead-singing drummer. This scene catches the band on stage halfway through a rocking song titled 'My Today My Tomorrow'. The audience is very much into the band and its music with heads bopping, scattered hands up in the air, and some of the audience singing the chorus along with Joe, except for Shelly and Cindy. Joe keeps looking over at her, leaning against a wall with her back to the band while she and Cindy are chatting with two guys.

The song ends and the crowd cheers. Joe gets up from behind his drums and walks over to Dave, The Threats' guitarist.

                    JOE
          Hey Dave, give me one of your
          guitars.

DAVE, Guitarist of The Threats. Long black hair that sticks up in every direction.

                    DAVE
          What? Why?

The crowd is still cheering...

                    JOE
          Hurry up!

Dave plugs another guitar into his amp and hands it to Joe.

                    DAVE
          What the heck are you doing?

Joe straps the guitar on and plays a chord to make sure it is working, then he addresses the audience.

                    JOE
          Thank you all so much for being such
          a great audience.
                    (MORE)

                                        (CONTINUED)

CONTINUED:

> JOE (cont'd)
> I'd like to play for you a new song I
> wrote this week, and I dedicate it to
> my fiance who is in the audience
> right now.

The crowd cheers and Shelly turns her head toward the stage, while her body still faces away. The rest of the band is wondering what is happening.

> DAVE
> (to Joe only)
> What the freak are we supposed to do?

> JOE
> (speaking to the band
> members)
> Follow along once you get where the
> song is going. (looks at keyboardist
> Jeff) Just play a tambourine, Jeff.

Joe then breaks into the song.

<PLAY SONG 'JUST YOU AND...'>

The audience is a bit taken back by the sudden change of style, looking around at each other, but eventually pays attention and shows fondness of the song. By the second verse, Dave adds some additional guitar work, and the bassist begins to follow by playing the root notes of the song. We see Jeff looking around the stage until he finds a tambourine near Joe's drums. Shelly turns her head away from the stage from the second verse on, where Joe can see that she has continued conversation with Cindy and the two guys. The song ends to a mild applause. Joe addresses the audience for the last time.

> JOE (cont'd)
> Thanks so much to those of you that
> actually listened to us. We're The
> Threats. Good-Night.

Joe hands Dave his guitar and heads toward the backstage door as the rest of the band tries to figure out what just happened, while they slowly take off their instruments, gazing at each other in a confused manner.

CUT TO:

INT. DRESSING ROOM - MOMENTS LATER

Joe is in the far corner, wiping the sweat from his hair with a towel, as the rest of the band members walk in. All are mumbling something about the strange way Joe ended the show. Dave walks over to Joe.

                    DAVE
          Dude, what was that?

                    JOE
          What? It was a new song.

                    DAVE
          I know it was a new song. One that
          the rest of us had never heard
          before.

                    JOE
               (sarcastically)
          Did you like it?

                    DAVE
          That's not the point. It's the
          biggest show of the year for us, we
          are blowing the roof off the place,
          and you end with a slow song that
          none of us have ever heard before?

Joe whips his towel against the wall.

                    JOE
          Don't worry, I'll save that song for
          my solo career.

                    DAVE
          What the hell has gotten into you?

Dave walks away from Joe to meet up with the rest of the band. Donny walks into the dressing room.

                    DONNY
          Killer show guys!

Donny continues walking past the band and over to Joe, now sitting in the corner.

                    DONNY (cont'd)
          Hey... What's up, man?

                    JOE
          What? You didn't like that new song
          either?

                                        (CONTINUED)

CONTINUED:

> DONNY
> No, it's not that. I thought it was
> pretty good. It was just unexpected,
> and kind-of a soft landing for what
> was such a high-energy show. I don't
> think I've ever seen you beat the
> drums as hard as you did tonight.
> Freakin' awesome.

> JOE
> Is all of the equipment moved?

> DONNY
> Yes, everything is toward the back of
> the stage like Keebler requested. He
> even gave me a hand to move things
> along because he wanted to have the
> stage all set before Joan Jett's
> stage manager came in from their
> tour-bus outside.

> JOE
> Did you see Shelly out there?

> DONNY
> Oh... Yeah, she told me to tell you
> "good show", and that she'll call you
> tomorrow.

> JOE
> Call me tomorrow?

> DONNY
> I guess her and Cindy are heading out
> to get a late-night breakfast?

> JOE
> Really? She left?

> DONNY
> It looked like she was heading out.
> You didn't know she was leaving after
> your set?

> JOE
> No. I thought she'd be hanging out
> with us like she always does. Figured
> she'd want to see Joan Jett, too.
> Were they with guys when they left?

CONTINUED:

                              DONNY
              I really didn't notice any guys
              leaving with them, but it is so
              packed out there that it is hard to
              know who is with who. Why? Are you
              worried about her meeting someone
              else?

The dressing room door opens abruptly and Joan Jett's stage
manager walks in and begins to speak abrasively.

JOAN JETT'S STAGE MANAGER, Husky-looking big guy with a
beard, wearing a sleeveless t-shirt, exposing large tattooed
arms.

                    JOAN JETT'S STAGE MANAGER
              Alright! I need ALL you guys back on
              that stage right now to move all your
              damned gear OFF the stage! I'm not
              going to have Joan and the band walk
              around all that crap while they are
              trying to get to their spots on the
              stage!

Joe gets up and walks toward the stage manager. Joe is
visibly upset.

                              JOE
              That freaking equipment is staying
              right the hell where it is. It is
              where we were told to place it
              because there is no room to put it
              anywhere else until the end of the
              freaking night.

                    JOAN JETT'S STAGE MANAGER
              Said who?!

                              JOE
              Said the guy that RUNS this stage,
              night after night, concert after
              concert, band after band! Billy Idol
              just played here last week, and The
              Ramones a few nights ago. They didn't
              have any problem walking around a few
              extra amps onstage. I'm sure that
              your band is capable of taking 3 or 4
              extra freaking steps on the way to
              their damned precious money-making
              spots!

                    JOAN JETT'S STAGE MANAGER
              Screw you!

                                             (CONTINUED)

CONTINUED:

Stage manager leaves, slamming the dressing room door.

> JOE
> Screw YOU, TOO!

Joe throws a pair of drum sticks, which hit the door just before the door opens again. Joe's sister, Jade, and her husband walk in.

> JADE
> What is going on?

The band begins to talk over each other about what just happened. Dave speaks to Joe.

> DAVE
> Dude... I don't think I've ever seen you this upset. You trying to get us banned from playing here or something?

> JOE
> Randy won't ban The Threats. Plus, we only did exactly what Keebler told us to do. I'm just freaking sick of taking crap from people.

> JADE
> Well, I don't know what is happening here, but Bill and I just wanted to let you know that it was a great show! Surprising ending. It was actually a nice change.

> JOE
> Whatever.

> JADE
> Bill and I are thinking about heading out. It's just way too crowded for us in here tonight.

> JOE
> Do you mind dropping me off on your way home?

> JADE
> You aren't going to catch Joan Jett's show? I know that you were excited to see her, Joey.

CONTINUED:

                    JOE
          I couldn't care less. Donny, can I
          count on you to pack my drums at the
          end of the night?

                    DONNY
          You got it, buddy.

                    JOE
          Thanks, man. All the beers that were
          mine in that cooler over there are
          now yours.

Joe picks up his sticks and walks out the dressing room
door. Jade and Bill give a puzzling wave to everyone in the
dressing room and exit.

                              FADE TO:

INT. MEXICAN RESTAURANT - EVENING

Shelly and Joe have finished a dinner, and are having small
talk. It is Joe's birthday.

                    SHELLY
          Well, it wasn't a burrito from Casa
          Vega, but I hope that you enjoyed it.

                    JOE
          I would have enjoyed a bowl of corn
          flakes, as long as you were in my
          company.

Several waiters and waitresses head over to Shelly and Joe's
table, singing a Happy Birthday song and clapping their
hands. One of the waitresses places a plate of deep-fried
ice cream with a lit candle on it in front of Joe. Several
people in the restaurant applaud.

                    JOE (cont'd)
          Thanks everyone!

                    SHELLY
          You always said that you wanted to
          try deep-fried ice cream.

                    JOE
          I know... It looks weird. Speaking of
          corn flakes, is that what this ice
          cream is covered with?

                                        (CONTINUED)

CONTINUED:

                         SHELLY
          I don't know. Hand me one of those
          spoons and I'll find out.

                         JOE
          When did you tell the waitress that
          it was my birthday?

                         SHELLY
          I can be sneaky and keep a secret
          when I want to.

                         JOE
          So, how does it taste?

                         SHELLY
          Mmmm... Really yummy. Here. Happy
          Birthday.

Shelly hands Joe a card. Joe opens it.

                         SHELLY (cont'd)
          Sorry that it's just a card. But I'll
          be picking you up something special
          from a far-away place.

                         JOE
          I really don't need anything, but
          what do you mean?

                         SHELLY
          I've been holding back on telling
          you, but I'll be going to England
          with Cindy for two weeks.

                         JOE
          England? Wow. When?

                         SHELLY
          Tomorrow.

                         JOE
          Tomorrow?! What?! Don't you need a
          passport?

                         SHELLY
          I got one a few weeks ago. Are you
          going to eat your deep-fried ice
          cream?

                         JOE
          What? You've known about this for
          weeks and didn't tell me? Why?
                         (MORE)

                                        (CONTINUED)

CONTINUED:
                    JOE (cont'd)
          And no, forget the ice cream. I'm not
          hungry now.

                    SHELLY
          See? I knew you'd be upset!

                    JOE
          Geez! It's not that I'm upset about
          you going, but it is quite a last
          minute surprise. Maybe I'm upset that
          you hid it from me for some reason.
          Now it all feels sneaky.

Shelly starts crying.

                    SHELLY
          I just want to go home now.

She gets up and grabs her pocket book.

                    JOE
          Sure, so you can pack for your secret
          excursion... although you've probably
          been packed for weeks now.

Joe gets up and squishes his napkin into what is left of his
deep-fried ice cream.

                    JOE (cont'd)
          Happy birthday to me!

                                        FADE TO:

INT. THE FAIRWAY BAR - LATE AFTERNOON (2 WEEKS LATER)

Joe and Donny are shooting pool.

                    DONNY
          Really? You haven't heard from her at
          all?

Joe aggressively breaks the balls to begin a new game.

                    JOE
          It's been almost two weeks. Not a
          single call.

                    DONNY
          When is she due to be back?

CONTINUED:

                    JOE
          Tomorrow. It's just that I don't know
          what to expect when I see her. I've
          been having nightmares about her
          finding someone new.

                    DONNY
          Come-on, man... You guys are engaged.
          She wouldn't hook up with anyone
          else.

                    JOE
          I'm telling you, something isn't
          right. I wrote a song about it this
          morning when I woke up. I had the
          worst feeling in my heart. I call it
          'Changing'. I just have this feeling
          that she is going to be a completely
          different person when I see her.

A couple walks into the bar, passing Joe and Donny.

                    COUPLE
          Hey guys.

                    DONNY
          How's it going?

                    COUPLE
          Doing good now that it's Miller time!
          Hey, where's your better half, Joe?

Joe pretends that he is concentrating on a shot.

                    DONNY
          It's an intense game. We'll catch up
          with you two in a few.

Joe takes a powerful shot, sending the cue ball sailing off
the table. Joe retrieves it, and holds onto it instead of
handing it to Donny.

                    JOE
          That's a line in the song I wrote
          today.

                    DONNY
          What are you talking about?

                    JOE
          What they just said... "Where's your
          better half?" I'm telling you, she is
          changing.

                                        (CONTINUED)

CONTINUED:

>   DONNY
>   Have you talked to Shelly's parents
>   since she left?

>   JOE
>   No. I don't want to bother them.

>   DONNY
>   Well, if it is bothering you like
>   this, you should stop by and visit
>   them.

Joe hands the cue ball to Donny and downs the half a beer
that is in his mug.

>   JOE
>   Finish the game solo?

>   DONNY
>   Good luck, man.

Joe exits the bar.

>   CUT TO:

INT. JOE'S CAR - MOMENTS LATER

<PLAY SONG 'CHANGING'>

Joe is driving in his car on the way to Shelly's house to
visit her parents. He looks nervous and bothered. This scene
shows cuts of him driving and scenes that Joe is imagining
during his drive... including: Shelly dancing at a nightclub
with guys... Shelly walking hand in hand down a romantic
cobble-stone street with a guy... Shelly having dinner on at
a side-walk cafe with a guy, sipping on wine and laughing...
Shelly in a guys' flat, kissing passionately as he leads her
into his bedroom.

Joe pulls up to Shelly's house. We see him take a deep
breath and ring the door-bell.

>   CUT TO:

INT. FANCY LIVING ROOM - EARLY EVENING

Joe is sitting on an antique sofa. Mrs. Cross walks in with
two glasses of wine, handing one to Joe.

                    MRS. CROSS
          I was going to call you. We're not
          really sure what is going on, but
          Shelly contacted us this morning and
          said that she and Cindy won't be
          returning tomorrow.

                    JOE
          What do you mean?

                    MRS. CROSS
          Again, we don't really have any
          details yet. She just said that she
          is having a good time and kept saying
          that she has grown up a lot since
          being out there. Mr. Cross wired her
          some money this afternoon so they'd
          have some cash to live on.

                    JOE
          Did she meet someone out there? I
          mean, what have they been doing?
          Where are they staying? I haven't
          heard from Shelly at all since I
          dropped her off the night before she
          left.

                    MRS. BENSON
          Mr. Cross and I don't know. She was
          quite vague. We are as concerned as
          you are. Her voice sounded hoarse,
          and her demeanor didn't sound like
          Shelly, but it's not like we can
          force her to come back.

Joe's eyes begin to tear up.

                    JOE
          I really don't get it.

                    MRS. CROSS
          I feel really bad for you, Joe.
          Shelly has to come back to Mr. Cross
          and me eventually, as we will always
          be her parents.
                    (MORE)

(CONTINUED)

CONTINUED:

                         MRS. CROSS (cont'd)
          I realize that you may not have that
          same fate, but I can tell you that I
          am hoping that you two will still be
          a couple when she returns. She is
          supposed to call us again tomorrow
          morning. I will try to get more
          information.

                         JOE
          Can you please ask her to call me
          right after she speaks with you? She
          can call me collect. I won't leave my
          place until I hear from her. PLEASE
          have her call me.

                         MRS. CROSS
          I can't promise that she will, but I
          will certainly ask her to. I'm so
          sorry, Joe.

                                        FADE TO:

INT. JOE'S APARTMENT - MORNING

Joe paces nervously. The phone on the wall rings. Joe
answers it.

                         JOE
          Hello

                         TELEPHONE OPERATOR
                    (English accent - off
                    screen)
          Hello. This is the operator. I have a
          collect call from Shelly Cross to Joe
          Silva.

                         JOE
          Yes, this is Joe

                         TELEPHONE OPERATOR
                    (off screen)
          Will you accept the charges?

                         JOE
          Yes

                         TELEPHONE OPERATOR
                    (off screen)
          OK. You are now being connected.

                                        (CONTINUED)

CONTINUED:

                              SHELLY
                    (hoarse voice - off
                     screen)
          Hello?

                              JOE
          Shelly. What is going on?

                              SHELLY
                    (off screen)
          Cindy and I are going to stay out
          here longer.

                              JOE
          Why?

                              SHELLY
                    (off screen)
          We're having fun, Joe.

                              JOE
          Why haven't you called or written
          since you left?

                              SHELLY
                    (off screen)
          I'm happy now, Joe.

                              JOE
          What does THAT mean? You weren't
          happy before?

                              SHELLY
                    (off screen)
          I've changed since being out here.

                              JOE
          Tell me where you are and I'll fly
          out there today so we can talk.

                              SHELLY
                    (off screen)
          No. I need my time.

                              JOE
          Please, Shelly. I miss and love you
          so much. Why are you doing this? Did
          you meet someone new?

                              SHELLY
                    (off screen)
          I want someone who wants to marry me
          now, not in a millennium.
                    (MORE)

                                        (CONTINUED)

CONTINUED:

> SHELLY (cont'd)
> Even Cindy's cousin Karen said that
> you don't treat me right.

> JOE
> Oh my God, Shelly. Karen doesn't even
> know me! Who the freak is SHE to
> judge me or us? I WOULD marry today.
> PLEASE tell me where you are so I can
> get to you. I will marry you on the
> spot.

> SHELLY
> (off screen - crying)
> I'm sorry. I don't need you anymore.

The phone goes dead.

> JOE
> Shelly?... SHELLY!

Joe hangs up the phone, hoping that it will ring again as he
paces back and forth a few times. He finally succumbs to the
notion that Shelly is breaking up with him, and he walks
over to the piano... in shock... and begins to write.

<PLAY SONG 'COLDEST DAY OF THE YEAR'>

                                                    FADE TO:

INT. THE LIVING ROOM MUSIC VENUE - LATE AFTERNOON

Joe is sitting at the bar with Randy, who is wearing his tan
over-sized-brim baseball cap, as usual. They are each having
a beer and conversing.

> RANDY
> I just can't believe it. You two were
> always together. I think that you
> two, as a couple, are almost as well
> known in Providence as your band is.

> JOE
> I know. I just don't get it, Randy.
> One day she is the closest person in
> the world to me, and I to her, then
> the next day I'm the last person on
> the planet that she wants to be with.

                                                    (CONTINUED)

CONTINUED:

                    RANDY
          When was the last time you spoke to
          her?

                    JOE
          It was a few weeks ago, when she
          called from England to tell me all of
          this. She hung up, and I haven't
          heard from her since.

                    RANDY
          It is true that time heals all
          wounds, but I'm sure that you don't
          want to hear that right now.

                    JOE
          Nothing will ever heal this wound.

                    RANDY
          Then NOW is the time for you to write
          your best song. Take all of that
          emotion you are feeling and turn it
          into the one love in your life that
          will NEVER die - your music.

                    JOE
          I might as well. It will give me
          something to do in seclusion, now
          that I don't want to go out and
          socialize anymore. I feel like such a
          loser.

                    RANDY
          Don't ever let me hear the word
          "loser" come out of your mouth again.
          You are the farthest thing from being
          a loser. You are a bright, talented,
          ambitious young man with a high
          capacity for love. Everybody loves
          you. Everybody. Like I always say,
          "The only thing we leave behind in
          this world..."

Joe finishes Randy's sentence.

                    JOE
          "...is our reputation."

                    RANDY
          You have one of the best reputations
          that I know of. Keep your chin up and
          you'll see a new sunrise eventually.

(CONTINUED)

CONTINUED:

                    JOE
          That's easier said than done right
          now.

                    RANDY
          Write your best song.

All of a sudden, Donny walks into the closed music venue,
looking for Joe.

                    DONNY
          THERE you are. Hi Randy. Joe, Shelly
          is back. I just ran into her at the
          gas station.

Joe stands up.

                    JOE
          And?

                    DONNY
          She said she got in last night, and
          that if you wanted to talk, you can
          swing by her parent's house at 5
          o'clock. After that, she'll be out
          with her folks.

                    RANDY
          It's already after 4. Get out of
          here.

                    JOE
          Thanks Randy... Thanks Donny!

Joe scurries out the door, as Donny takes his seat next to
Randy.

                                        FADE TO:

INT. SHELLY'S BEDROOM - HALF HOUR LATER

Joe is standing in the middle of the room, not knowing what
to do or say. Shelly is facing the wall, also not saying
anything. She finally turns around and holds out her hand,
which has her engagement ring sitting on her palm.

                    SHELLY
          It's only fair that you would get
          this back.

Joe takes the ring from her palm.

                                        (CONTINUED)

CONTINUED:

                    JOE
          That's all you have to say?

Joe waits 30 seconds. Shelly is staring at the ground,
saying nothing. Joe puts the ring in his pocket and heads
toward the door to leave. Shelly darts to the door ahead of
Joe and closes it before he can walk out of the room.

                    SHELLY
          I don't want to lose you.

                    JOE
          Then don't.

The two begin to kiss, and make their way over to Shelly's
bed. The two become embraced in passion for a few minutes,
until Joe notices Shelly's tummy contracting as if she is
crying. He looks at her face and sees tears streaming from
her eyes, and pulls away.

                    JOE (cont'd)
          Did you fall in love with someone in
          England?

                    SHELLY
          No.

                    JOE
          Is there someone in England that you
          like?

                    SHELLY
          I liked a lot of people in England.

Joe's eyes water as he buttons his shirt back up.

                    SHELLY (cont'd)
          Don't think that I won't miss you.

                    JOE
          I'll miss you, too.

                    SHELLY
          I hope that we can always be friends.

Joe says nothing as he leaves Shelly's room for the last
time.

                              FADE TO:

INT. JOE'S BEDROOM - 3:00AM

Joe is twisting and turning in his bed, and is having an obviously tough time staying asleep. He eventually turns on a night-stand light, gets up to grab his acoustic guitar, and returns to his bed. Joe sits cross-legged in his bed as he begins to strum a few chords. He reaches for the pad of paper and pen that sits on his night-stand and he scratches some lyrics onto the paper.

<PLAY SONG 'FOREVER THERE FOR YOU' (ACOUSTIC VERSION)>

This scene shows various cuts of Joe walking around his bedroom, looking at photos of Shelly and himself, and walking back to add more lyrics. Whenever the scene shows a photo of Shelly and Joe, it morphs into a live scene from where the photo was taken (for instance, we may see Joe look at a shot from Disneyland, then his memory shows them on a ride together, eating ice-cream while watching the Disney parade, and laughing while they have their photo taken with Goofy & Mickey Mouse). We see several photos/live scenes while the song plays and Joe goes back & forth from photo to note pad to photo, etc. We finally see the sun peeking through the shades as a new day begins. Joe peeks out to look at it, turns off the light on the nightstand, and crawls back into bed, pulling the covers over his head.

                                        CUT TO:

EXT. JOE'S APARTMENT - LATE MORNING

Donny is knocking at the door. He waits and receives no response. He knocks again, but louder. Still no response. We see that he is getting nervous. He begins to look into windows that don't have the shades drawn, but sees no evidence of life inside. Feeling more nervous that Joe might have done something to harm himself, he notices that one of the windows is unlocked. Donny takes his keys out of his pocket and cuts the screen enough so that he can get his fingers in to pull the latches and raise the screen. He then raises the window and hoists himself up and through the window and lands inside on a pile of empty beer cans, creating a clatter. Still, there is no evidence of life inside the house except for his own. He looks even more nervous as he slowly heads to Joe's bedroom and opens the door. He looks in to see that there is a body under the covers.

                                        (CONTINUED)

CONTINUED:

                    DONNY
                 (in a low voice)
          Oh, man...

Donny slowly reaches to pull the covers back when Joe wakes
up in a startle, which rattles Donny.

                    JOE
          AAGGHH!

                    DONNY
          AAGGHH!

Donny jumps back a few steps.

                    JOE
          What the hell!?

                    DONNY
          What the hell is right! Dude, I've
          been calling you all morning. You
          look like shit.

                    JOE
          Thanks for that. SECURITY! How did
          you get in?

                    DONNY
          Climbed through a window. I was
          worried about you. Oh, and I think I
          owe you a screen.

                    JOE
          Who cares. Smash the freaking window,
          too. May as well add that to my heart
          being freaking shattered.

                    DONNY
          What happened when you saw Shelly
          last night?

                    JOE
          Not a whole lot. She gave me back the
          ring... Then she told me she didn't
          want to lose me... Then we got
          intimate until ice-cold tears ran
          down her face and froze her heart. I
          got the old "I hope that we can still
          be friends" bull.

                    DONNY
          Man, I'm sorry bro.

(CONTINUED)

CONTINUED:

> JOE
>
> I don't freaking get it. It's over
> just like that. One trip to England
> and 6 and a half years gone like
> they're minutes to spare.

Joe takes a framed photo of Shelly and him from his
nightstand and whips it across the room, smashing it against
the far wall.

> DONNY
>
> Come-on. Take a shower and get
> dressed. I'm taking you out of here.

Donny opens the shade, allowing a flood of light to pour
into the room. Joe hides from it like a vampire, pulling the
covers back over his head.

> JOE
> (muffled under the
> covers)
> I'm not going anywhere.

> DONNY
>
> You HAVE to come. I've got two
> tickets for today's Red Sox game.

Joe lifts his head from under the covers, squinting his
eyes.

> JOE
>
> Seriously? How'd you get tickets for
> today's game? The Sox are playing the
> Yankees and the series has been sold
> out since the beginning of the
> season.

> DONNY
> (flashing the tickets)
> Randy gave them to me last night. He
> said that you'd need to go to the
> game more than he would. Hurry up,
> it's a matinee game.

> JOE
>
> Wow... Really?... Randy looks forward
> to that series every year.

Joe gets up, grabs a towel from the closet, and leaves the
room.

DISSOLVE TO:

EXT. FENWAY PARK IN BOSTON - MID AFTERNOON

Joe and Donny make their way down the 1st base bleacher
stairs toward their seats, both carrying hot dogs and sodas,
and wearing sunglasses. Two attractive females are making
their way up the stairs, checking out Joe & Donny as they
pass. Donny turns back toward them to take another look, but
Joe continues to look ahead the entire time.

                    DONNY
          Did you see them checking us out?
          That's what you have to look forward
          to. You can be with any girl you want
          now.

                    JOE
          Can I?

                    DONNY
          It looks that way to me.

                    JOE
          Yeah, well the only girl I want just
          kicked me out of her life.

They find their seats, which are at the end of an isle. Joe
slips into the isle first and Donny takes the end seat. The
game is already under way, and Fenway Park is packed except
for the two seats next to Joe.

                    DONNY
          Hey, maybe those two hot chicks are
          sitting next to you.

                    JOE
          Yeah, well, if they are, you and I
          can switch seats so you can be next
          to them. I have no interest.

The two begin unwrapping their hot dogs as they settle into
the game, when a middle-aged English couple arrive at their
row.

                    ENGLISH MAN
                 (in English accent)
          Pardon us, please... Cheers.

Donny and Joe juggle their food and sodas as they make room
for the couple to pass. The woman seems to be scolding the
man as she laboriously makes her way to her seat while
passing Joe.

(CONTINUED)

CONTINUED:

                    ENGLISH WOMAN
                 (in English accent
                 and snooty tone)
            Honestly, Stuart, what are we even
            bloody doing here? This isn't like
            Cricket at all.

The English couple sit the two seats next to Joe. We hear
"Batting next for Boston"... over the stadium's speakers.

                    DONNY
            Remember how that was your dream when
            we were kids? For you to step up to
            the plate here at Fenway?

Donny bites into his hot dog, watching the game, and not
noticing that Joe has tears streaming down his face from
behind his sunglasses.

                              FADE TO:

INT. THE THREATS REHEARSAL SPACE - 2 WEEKS LATER - EVENING

Band members and girlfriends are arriving, getting their
equipment turned on and instruments tuned. Jeff pulls Joe
aside.

                    JEFF
            Hey, man. I'm not really sure how to
            break this to you.

                    JOE
            Dude, everything in my life has been
            broken... My trust, my heart, what's
            left?

                    JEFF
            Well, I was talking with Cindy...

                    JOE
            Why the heck do you even TALK to
            Cindy, anyway?

                    JEFF
            I'm sorry, but I've known her a long
            time. Anyway, she told me that a guy
            that Shelly met in England is here
            now, and that they are getting an
            apartment together.

CONTINUED:

                  JOE
Are you kidding me? They hung out for
a few weeks in England while she was
on vacation. He then jumps the ocean
and they are moving in together?
Where is he staying now?

                  JEFF
At the Cross's house.

Joe walks over to the couch and sits down, shaking his head.

                  JOE
Holy crap... I didn't love anyone in
England, my ass... Holy crap.

                  JEFF
At least you know now that it wasn't
you... That there WAS someone else.

                  JOE
Boy, that's not really making me feel
any better.

                  JEFF
Come-on... You've got to move on...
Let's play.

                  JOE
I'm not playing now. I can hardly
breath.

Dave chimes in from the opposite side of the room.

                  DAVE
Dude, if we don't play tonight, I
ain't playing the show on Friday.

                  JOE
Really? You won't play at The Vet's
Auditorium, opening for The Hooters
in front of 2,300 people? You'll be
there.

                  DAVE
Watch me NOT be there.

Joe walks behind his drums, sits down and adjusts his
microphone.

                  JOE
Thanks for your freaking sympathy,
Dave.

(CONTINUED)

CONTINUED:

MIKE, The Threats' bassist. Long hair, ripped jeans and
plain black T-shirt

                    MIKE
          Joe, I'm really sorry that you're
          going through this. I didn't feel
          that it was any of my business so I
          haven't said anything yet. Plus, I
          just kind-of figured you two would
          get back together. Sucks, man.

Joe puts his closed fist out toward Mike, and Mike connects
with his fist.

                    MIKE (cont'd)
          You'll get through this. Life is full
          of surprises. It's hard for any of us
          to know what the future holds, or
          when we are getting it right.

Joe picks up his sticks and speaks into the microphone.

                    JOE
          Alright... First song... "Getting It
          Right"

Joe breaks into the song and the rest of the band follows.

<PLAY SONG 'GETTING IT RIGHT'>

During the song, we see various cuts. First of the band
rehearsing, then packing the van, then setting up on the
stage of the large and empty Veteran's Memorial Auditorium,
and then finishing the song in concert in front of the sold-
out audience, ending in a loud eruption of cheering.

                                        DISSOLVE TO:

INT. DRESSING ROOM - MOMENTS LATER

Joe is in front of a fancy dressing room mirror, drying his
sweat-drenched hair with a hair dryer and drinking a beer.
Don walks in, followed by a young woman. Joe doesn't notice
or hear Donny, at first, over the sound of the hair dryer.

                    DONNY
          Joe... JOE!

                                        (CONTINUED)

CONTINUED:

Joe, a bit startled, turns off the hair dryer.

                    JOE
          Oh... Hey... Sorry.

                    DONNY
          Great show, man. This woman is from
          L.A., and she wants to speak with
          you. I'll let you two chat while I
          see what food is left in the
          hospitality room.

Donny exits the posh dressing room.

BIBI, Woman in her mid-20's, Curly big black hair, wearing a
pant-suit.

                    BIBI
          Hi. My name is Bibi. I'm in town from
          Los Angeles and decided to catch this
          concert by The Hooters and was very
          impressed with your band's
          performance as an opening act.

Joe extends his hand and Bibi shakes it.

                    JOE
          Nice to meet you, Bibi. Thanks for
          the compliment. It's a great crowd
          out there.

                    BIBI
          I'm with Silver Mountain
          Entertainment. We manage many well-
          known acts and artists. Here is my
          card in-case you'd like to send us a
          promotional package of your band.

                    JOE
          I will do that. You just saw us
          perform, isn't that enough for you to
          know if you'd like to manage us or
          not?

                    BIBI
          Well, we usually only manage acts
          that are already signed to a label
          and established. I don't do the
          signing, but I'm willing to pass it
          along.

                                        (CONTINUED)

CONTINUED:

> JOE
> I'll mail one out to you this week.
> Is this your phone number on the
> card?

> BIBI
> It sure is. Well, I'll give you your
> privacy back. Want to catch a drink
> after The Hooters play?

> JOE
> I'd really like to, Bibi, but I've
> got too much to do with packing our
> equipment and getting everything back
> to our rehearsal space. I'm in Los
> Angeles fairly often, so maybe a
> rain-check?

> BIBI
> Sounds good to me.

FADE TO:

INT. JOE'S APARTMENT - AFTERNOON (2 WEEKS LATER)

Phone is ringing and Joe picks it up.

> JOE
> Hello

> BIBI
> Hi, Joe?

> JOE
> This is.

> BIBI
> This is Bibi from Silver Mountain.
> Hey, your demo sounds really good.
> I'll pass it along, but no promises.

> JOE
> Thanks Bibi.

> BIBI
> Hey, I know that you mentioned
> traveling to L.A. Often, but have you
> ever thought about moving out here? I
> think it would be so much better for
> your music career than being in Rhode
> Island.

(CONTINUED)

CONTINUED:

                    JOE
I agree, and yes, I have thought
about it more than once.

                    BIBI
Well, if you decide to make the leap,
let me know. I could definitely get
you a job working at one of our act's
studios or something.

                    JOE
Wow. Thanks. Let me think on that and
get back to you, OK?

                    BIBI
Of course... Whenever you decide.

                    DISSOLVE TO:

INT. THE LIVING ROOM MUSIC VENUE - EVENING

Joe and Donny are sitting at the bar in the Living Room.
They are having a beer, laughing and having fun, while
waiting for a band to take the stage. It is fairly loud in
the venue. We see Donny tap Joe's shoulder and motion Joe to
look at the entrance-way. Joe's laughter and smile turns
into a frown as he sees Shelly paying the doorman for
herself and her guy from England. Joe gets up and heads for
Randy's office. He knocks and the door opens.

                    CUT TO:

INT. RANDY'S OFFICE - MOMENTS LATER

Randy is seated behind a desk that is loaded with cassette
tapes, CD's, band promotional photos, etc., as Joe is pacing
back and forth in front of Randy, who is wearing his
trademark tan baseball cap with the over-sized brim.

                    JOE
I mean, how can she even freaking
come here, never mind bringing him
with her?... This is MY freaking hang
out.

                    RANDY
I know it isn't easy, Joe. Been
there, done that. My ex still comes
here, and I OWN the place. I mean it
when I say that the healing takes
time, and time IS the healer.
                    (MORE)

                    (CONTINUED)

CONTINUED:

              RANDY (cont'd)
         It has only been a few months.
         Eventually, you may still say "What
         the heck?", but you won't feel that
         gut-wrenching pain that you're
         feeling right now.

              JOE
         But that pain only gets worse with
         time, it seems.

              RANDY
         You know how to instantly make it
         less painful? Walk right out there to
         both of them. Say hello to Shelly and
         hold your hand out to her new guy.
         Shake his hand and introduce
         yourself. You'll be surprised at what
         forgiveness can do. Plus, you'll
         leave a good reputation in your wake.

              JOE
         I'm not ready for that. As a matter
         of fact, I think I may move out to
         L.A. soon. I've got a few
         opportunities out there that I should
         explore instead of hanging around
         here and watching Shelly parade her
         new guy around. Plus, I may have
         already written my best song. I'll
         have a better shot of making
         something out of it in Hollywood.

                             DISSOLVE TO:

INT. THE THREATS REHEARSAL SPACE - EVENING

The band is gathered in conversation.

              DAVE
         But, we are getting bigger and bigger
         around here. We just played the Vet's
         Auditorium and blew the roof off the
         place.

              JOE
         We're big fish in a little pond. I'm
         telling you, if we were playing the
         same shows in L.A., we'd be signed to
         a record label by now.

                                        (CONTINUED)

CONTINUED:

                    DAVE
          I'm not doing it man. Plus, I've got
          to take care of my mother. I can't
          move to the other side of the
          country.

                    JOE
          Well, I can't argue with that, but
          I'm definitely going whether you guys
          come with me or not.

                    MIKE
          I can't move either. Dude, this
          sucks.

                    JEFF
          I've got nothing holding me back.
          I'll move out there with you. It'll
          be an adventure for sure.

                              DISSOLVE TO:

EXT. JOE'S MOTHER'S HOUSE - AFTERNOON

Jeff and Joe pull up in an SUV, towing a U-Haul trailer, to
the curb outside Joe's mother's house. Joe's family has
gathered on the front lawn to say goodbye. We see Joe
hugging a few of his sisters, and his mother, who is crying.
Jade calls to Joe from the front door of the house.

                    JADE
          Joey! You have a phone call!

Joe enters the house.

                    JOE
          Who is it?

                    JADE
          It was kind of loud, but I think that
          it's Donny.

Joe takes the phone receiver from Jane and speaks into it.

                    JOE
          Who else is doing this?

                    DONNY
          Hey, Joe, You'll have to speak up, it
          is kind of loud in here.

                                        (CONTINUED)

CONTINUED:

> JOE
> WHO ELSE IS DOING THIS?!

> DONNY
> Ha Ha! Only you, my friend.

> JOE
> Where are you? I thought you were
> coming here to say goodbye and have
> one last beer with me.

> DONNY
> Dude, I lost track of time and am in
> the middle of a pool game at The
> Fairway. Shelly and Cindy are here
> and just bought a round of drinks so
> I don't want to be rude and just
> leave.

> JOE
> You are hanging out with Shelly?
> Yeah, I wouldn't want you to be rude
> or anything.

Joe hangs up the phone and heads back outside. Jeff is
chatting with Joe's family on the lawn.

> JOE (cont'd)
> Alright... Hollywood or bust! You'd
> better all come visit us!

Joe gives his mother a last hug, then goes to get into the
SUV.

> JADE
> Hey Joey... What about me?

Joe turns around and hugs Jade.

> JOE
> Oh, Jade. I'm sorry. I'm going to
> miss you most of all.

Jade hands him an envelope.

> JOE (cont'd)
> What's this?

> JADE
> It's an open-ended plane ticket, just
> in-case you need to come home at any
> time.

(CONTINUED)

CONTINUED:

Joe slaps the envelope against his other palm as he gets
into the passenger-side of the vehicle.

                JOE
        Thanks, Jade... Love you.

Joe closes the door and the SUV pulls away. He opens the
envelope and reads the card that Jade gave to him...

"Dear Joey,
I hope that you always follow the SUN, and that it leads you
on a journey through your dream. I'll be with you in spirit
with every song that you sing!
Love,
Jade"

                        DISSOLVE TO:

INT. JEFF'S SUV - LATE AFTERNOON

Jeff is driving while Joe stares out the window. We see them
pass a 'Welcome to New York' sign on the road, and several
crosses along the highway.

                JEFF
        OK, it's been over three hours and
        you haven't said a word. Sad about
        leaving Rhode Island?

                JOE
        I'm actually sad about all of these
        crosses that I keep seeing along the
        highway. Evidence of so much death,
        yet most who pass them will never
        know anything about any of the people
        they represent.

                JEFF
        Is that all that is bothering you?

                JOE
        That is all that is making me sad.
        What makes me pissed is Donny not
        being there to say goodbye, but
        rather at The Fairway having fun with
        Shelly and Cindy.

CONTINUED:

                    JEFF
          You need to let that crap go. It
          sucks that you and Shelly aren't an
          item anymore, but all of us have been
          friends with Shelly and Cindy for at
          least as many years that you two were
          together. You can't expect every
          friendship that Shelly had to end all
          of a sudden.

                    JOE
          Why? That's what freaking happened to
          me. All of those years together and
          BOOM... I don't exist to her anymore
          and she's living with another guy...
          All of a sudden.

                    JEFF
          Come-on, man... Forgive everyone and
          you'll feel better. You can't be
          distracted with hurt and anger like
          this. You're on a mission. Don't let
          bad thoughts derail you.

Joe continues to stare out the window as they pass a cluster
of three more crosses along the road. Joe reaches behind his
seat and grabs a travel-size guitar and a pad of paper, then
begins strumming.

<PLAY SONG 'CROSSES ON THE HIGHWAY'>

While the song plays, Jeff and Joe pass several 'Welcome
To...' state signs, and many, many various crosses dotting
the highway... Pennsylvania (we pass Amish horse-drawn
buggies going down the road, past crosses), Illinois (we see
the city of Chicago in the background while passing
crosses), Kansas (we see crosses and farmland with round
bales of hay, which seem to go on forever), Colorado (snow
is falling on crosses that Joe & Jeff pass, with mountains
in the distance), Arizona (crosses line a straight highway
that stretches countless miles to the horizon, with cactus &
buttes on either side), California (we see crosses on the
highway, then a pan up to get a view of the Hollywood sign).

                                        FADE TO:

INT. JOE AND JEFF'S APARTMENT - AFTERNOON

Jeff is sitting on a box-filled, furniture-less living-room
floor in front of a pizza box, eating a slice. Joe is
struggling to carry a heavy over-sized box through the
apartment door. Jeff continues to watch as Joe gets his
finger caught between the box and the door.

                    JOE
              OUCH!

Joe drops the box, and attempts to shake the pain off his
hand.

                    JEFF
              Dude, that's my stuff in there!

Joe notices that his finger is bleeding, and heads over to
the roll of paper towels near Jeff to wrap his finger.

                    JOE
              Yeah? Well it's my finger that is
              bleeding from carrying your crap.

Joe looks down and sees two slices of pizza in the pizza box
as Jeff closes it.

                    JOE (cont'd)
              Jeff, I'll give you a dollar for one
              of those slices. I'm starving.

Jeff gets up, carrying the box over to the kitchen counter.

                    JEFF
              No. I'm saving them for later. Do you
              have the keys to the SUV?

                    JOE
              Yeah. Why, are you heading out?

                    JEFF
              Not tonight.

                    JOE
              Would you mind if I use it? That girl
              Bibi invited me out to see some
              singer that her agency is thinking
              about managing. She's supposed to set
              me up with a job.

(CONTINUED)

CONTINUED:

                    JEFF
I'll need to keep it here. I'm
leaving to go skiing at my family's
vacation place in Utah tomorrow and I
might pack it tonight.

                    JOE
Oh, really? That kind-of sucks. I
just dropped-off the U-Haul trailer
and got the SUV washed. What if I
help you pack it in the morning?

                    JEFF
No. I'm going to pack it tonight.

                    JOE
I guess I'll call and have her pick
me up. How long are you going to Utah
for?

                    JEFF
Not sure. Two weeks or so?

                    JOE
Two weeks?! Don't you need to find a
job here?

                    JEFF
Not right away. My Dad will be
sending me checks.

                    JOE
Do you mind if I use your bike to get
around while you're away?

                    JEFF
I'm taking my bike.

                    JOE
To the mountain? All the roads will
be snow-covered. You won't be riding
any bike there.

                    JEFF
I'm taking it.

                              FADE TO:

EXT. OUTSIDE BIBI'S CONDO - EARLY EVENING

Bibi and Joe get out of her sports car and walk toward the
front door of her condo.

                              (CONTINUED)

CONTINUED:

>   BIBI
>   I hope that you don't mind us
>   stopping here first. I forgot the
>   tickets for the event in my room.

>   JOE
>   Not at all. I just feel bad that you
>   had to drive over the hills to Studio
>   City to pick me up, then all the way
>   back here. It must be cool living in
>   Beverly Hills. I love this section of
>   Los Angeles.

>   BIBI
>   Yeah. I never get tired of it.

Bibi unlocks the door and the two walk in.

                                        CUT TO:

INT. BIBI'S BEDROOM - MOMENTS LATER

Bibi is looking through her nightstand drawer.

>   BIBI
>   Come on in.

Joe steps into the room and is taken back as he notices one
of the promotional photos of himself that was included in
the music package he sent to Bibi is hanging on her wall
over her bed's headboard.

>   BIBI (cont'd)
>   So, what do you think of my place?

>   JOE
>   I like it. Sort-of classic Hollywood,
>   yet modern at the same time.

We see that Joe feels awkward about the photo being on her
wall, and pretends that he didn't see it as he exits the
room and stands near the front door.

>   BIBI
>   Found 'em!

Bibi waves the tickets in the air as she also heads toward
the front door.

                                        CUT TO:

EXT. SANTA MONICA BOULEVARD - EVENING

Bibi and Joe are walking on the sidewalk. Bibi goes to hold
Joe's hand and Joe acts like he is reaching for his wallet,
as he places his hand in his leather sports-jacket.

                    JOE
          How much do I owe you for the
          tickets?

                    BIBI
          This is an event strictly for the
          music industry. Invite only, so there
          is no charge for the tickets.

                    JOE
          What's the singer's name again?

                    BIBI
          Sheryl Crow. Her first record is
          about to come out, and there is a lot
          of buzz in the industry about her.

Bibi and Joe arrive at the door of the venue. We hear
singing and acoustic guitar coming through the door.

                    BIBI (cont'd)
          Looks like we're late... Follow me.

Joe follows Bibi through the small and crowded venue. Bibi
goes straight to the open bar and asks for two beers.

                    JOE
          How did you know what to order for
          me?

                    BIBI
          I've been in your dressing room,
          remember?

The two begin to drink their beers while Sheryl Crow
addresses the gathered crowd of music industry people.

                    SHERYL CROW
          I'd like to thank all of you so much
          for being here tonight. Most of all,
          thank you for believing in me. I
          can't believe that my dreams are
          coming true. I am having so much fun,
          and as my last song suggests, all I
          want to do is have some fun!

                                        (CONTINUED)

CONTINUED:

Bibi notices Joe becoming engaged with Sheryl's stage presence.

                    JOE
          Should we move up closer to the
          stage?

Bibi puts her empty beer bottle on the bar, grabbing Joe's arm as she heads for the door. Joe unsuccessfully tries to swig his beer down before reaching the door, then hands the half-full bottle to the doorman while still being dragged away by Bibi. We see the two of them walking on the sidewalk back toward Bibi's car.

                    JOE (cont'd)
          Why did we leave so soon?

                    BIBI
          My job is done for the night. I
          showed my face.

                    JOE
          Are you guys going to manage her?

                    BIBI
          Probably not.

                    JOE
          Why not? I thought she sounded great,
          what little I heard of her.

                    BIBI
          Our agency is ultra selective. I'm
          going to take you to see a killer
          band right now at Club Lingerie. They
          are good friends of mine.

                    JOE
          Do you folks manage them?

                    BIBI
          You still have a lot to learn about
          L.A... This isn't Providence. It
          takes an awful lot to rise to the top
          here, and a lot of it has nothing to
          do with talent.

                                        DISSOLVE TO:

INT. CLUB LINGERIE - MOMENTS LATER

Bibi is holding Joe's hand, leading him through the crowded music venue to the dressing room door at the back of the club. We see Joe looking down at his hand now and then and can tell that he is uncomfortable. They enter the room to cheers from the band and their guests, shouting "Bibi's here! Hey Bibi!". Bibi continues to hold his hand once inside the dressing room, and begins introducing him to everyone.

                    BIBI
          Hey everyone! This is Joe, the guy
          that I've been telling you about.

One of the band members grabs a couple of beers from a tub of ice and hands them to Bibi and Joe, allowing an excuse for Joe to reclaim his hand from Bibi. He opens the bottle and raises it in the air.

                    JOE
          Cheers everyone! Nice to meet you
          all!

Bibi then places her hand on Joe's back, giving a gentle rub.

                    JOE (cont'd)
          Bibi, do you know where the Men's
          Room is?

                    BIBI
          Yeah, take a right outside the
          dressing room door and it will be the
          last door on your right. I'll wait
          for you in here.

                    JOE
          Sounds good.

                                        CUT TO:

INT. MEN'S ROOM - MOMENTS LATER

Joe is pacing a bit until someone walks by him and enters a stall. Walking over to the sink, Joe splashes water on his face and rolls out some paper towel to dry with. He leans back against the wall, scratching his head. The door opens again as another person walks in. He sees Bibi through the open door, who is looking in at him. Joe walks out to face her.

                                        (CONTINUED)

CONTINUED:

                    BIBI
          The band is getting ready to take the
          stage, so I figured I'd wait for you
          here. Are you OK?

                    JOE
          Actually, I'm not feeling all that
          great. I should probably head back to
          my apartment and get some rest. I
          haven't really stopped, or eaten well
          since I got into town, but I don't
          want to end your night too early. I
          can take a cab back.

                    BIBI
          Are you kidding me? I'm not letting
          you take a cab. I'll drive you. Come
          on.

Bibi grabs Joe's hand again, leading him back through the
crowd.

                                        CUT TO:

INT. BIBI'S CAR - MOMENTS LATER

Bibi and Joe are sitting in her car, which is parked outside
of Joe's apartment.

                    BIBI
          So, should I come up?

                    JOE
          I probably wouldn't be very good
          company, considering how I feel. I'm
          sorry to cut the night short.

                    BIBI
          Then how about a good-night kiss?

Bibi leans over toward Joe.

                    JOE
          Bibi, you know that I think you're a
          really cool girl. It just seems that
          every time a relationship between a
          guy and a girl ends, they aren't
          really friends any more. Considering
          we will be working together, I don't
          think it would be the best idea for
          us to get romantic, ya know?
                    (MORE)

                                        (CONTINUED)

CONTINUED:

                    JOE (cont'd)
          I do think that we would make awesome
          friends, though.

Bibi leans back in her seat, looking disappointed.

                    BIBI
          I guess you're right. Well, let me
          talk to my higher-ups at work and
          I'll get back to you. I hope that you
          feel better.

                    JOE
          Thanks for understanding, Bibi.

                                        FADE TO:

INT. JOE AND JEFF'S APARTMENT - MORNING 5 DAYS LATER

Joe is on the phone, listening to several repeated ring
tones. Finally, an answering machine picks up.

                    BIBI'S ANSWERING MACHINE
               (off screen)
          Hi, This is Bibi. I can't get to the
          phone right now but please leave a
          message... BEEP

                    JOE
          Hi Bibi. This is Joe calling. Just
          checking in to learn if you had a
          chance to speak with your boss about
          the job. Thankfully, I'm feeling much
          better, and hoping that all is well
          with you, too. I look forward to your
          response.

                                        DISSOLVE TO:

INT. JOE AND JEFF'S APARTMENT - EVENING

Joe is on the phone again.

                    BIBI'S ANSWERING MACHINE
               (off screen)
          BEEP

                    JOE
          Hi Bibi. It's Joe. I'm not sure if my
          last message went through a few days
          ago. Just wanted to check in with you
          about the job.
               (MORE)

                                        (CONTINUED)

CONTINUED:

                       JOE (cont'd)
       I'm looking forward to it. Please
       give me a call. Hope all is well.

                              DISSOLVE TO:

INT. JOE AND JEFF'S APARTMENT - AFTERNOON

We see Joe looking a bit disheveled, wearing sweatpants.

                    BIBI'S ANSWERING MACHINE
       BEEP

                       JOE
       Hello Bibi. I'm guessing that you
       have been getting my messages.
       Wondering why you haven't called back
       yet, seeing that it has been a few
       weeks that I've been trying to reach
       you. Please call me back so I know
       what is going on OK? Thanks, Bibi.

Joe begins to walk down the hall to his bedroom when the
phone rings. He stumbles over one of the several boxes in
the hallway that each have "DRUM" written on them in back
magic marker, as he clumsily hurries to answer the phone.

                     JOE (cont'd)
       Hello, Bibi?

                     JOE'S MOTHER
          (off screen)
       It's your mother.

                     JOE
       Oh... Hi Mom.

                     JOE'S MOTHER
          (off screen)
       Well, don't sound so excited.

                     JOE
       I'm sorry. You caught me off-guard. I
       was expecting a call from someone.

                     JOE'S MOTHER
          (off screen)
       How's the new job going?

                     JOE
       I think it starts next week.

                              (CONTINUED)

CONTINUED:

                         JOE'S MOTHER
                    (off screen)
               Have you been eating well?

                         JOE
               I've been eating well enough... Mom,
               I hate to rush you off, but do you
               mind if I call you back later? The
               call I am waiting on is about the
               job.

                         JOE'S MOTHER
                    (off screen)
               Of course... But don't forget about
               your mother.

                         JOE
               You know I won't Mom. Love you!

                         JOE'S MOTHER
                    (off screen)
               Love you too.

Joe hangs the phone up and heads back to his room. The phone
rings again and he darts back toward the phone, and again
trips on the same box. Joe answers the phone.

                         JOE
               Hi, Bibi?

                                        CUT BACK &
                                        FORTH BETWEEN
                                        JOE IN HIS
                                        APARTMENT AND
                                        RANDY SITTING
                                        AT HIS DESK IN
                                        HIS OFFICE

As usual, Randy is wearing his tan baseball hat with the
over-sized brim.

                         RANDY
               Wow, you're already hooking up with
               the chicks? I told you time would
               heal all.

                         JOE
               Ha Ha! Hey Randy. No, I'm NOT hooking
               up with the chicks, which is probably
               why I don't have a job right now.

                                             (CONTINUED)

CONTINUED:

                        RANDY

I thought that someone was giving you a job out there in the music industry?

                        JOE

Yes, I thought so too... That's who Bibi is. We went out a few weeks ago to an industry event and she kept making advances toward me. At the end of the night I explained that I thought it was best if we just remained friends, considering we'd be working together, and that's the last I've seen of her. I keep leaving messages but she isn't returning my calls.

                        RANDY
                    (off screen)
What are you going to do?

                        JOE

Looks like I'll hit the street looking for work. Any kind of work.

                        RANDY

What about your friends at 'Married with Children'? Didn't they say they could get you a job on the studio lot?

                        JOE

Yes, but we're good friends and I don't want to put them on the spot to get me hired, you know? I'll find something. I'm just nervous about money running out too soon, never mind finding a rehearsal studio where I can set up my drums and put a new band together. They are all still in boxes, which is making my soul suffocate and starve.

                        RANDY

Well, in the meantime, don't be too proud to get yourself on food-stamps. You need to eat and keep your body healthy, especially as you go through this stress.

CONTINUED:

>   JOE
>   Got to eat... Now you sound like my
>   mother. I don't want to go on food-
>   stamps, Randy. That's not me.

>   RANDY
>   Yeah, well that wasn't me either, but
>   there was a time in my life when I
>   had no choice. Sometimes it is good
>   for a person to face struggles and be
>   humbled in life. Plus, nobody else
>   needs to know. It won't damage your
>   reputation, Joe.

>   JOE
>   Thanks Randy, but I'll land a job
>   soon.

<PLAY SONG 'SURVIVE'>

                                        FADE TO:

Here we see several clips of Joe walking in and out of
various businesses, holding a binder and handing out
resumes, talking to an executive sitting behind a desk and
other various hiring folks like store managers. He is
constantly facing rejection. These businesses include a
large corporation, musical instrument shop, book store,
restaurant, gas station and pet store. We also see Joe in
line at a job fair, and though he is dressed nicely, it is
apparent that his longer-than-most hair makes him stand out
among the dozens of "well groomed" employee candidates in
line.

                                        FADE TO:

INT. LENNY'S APARTMENT - LATE MORNING

Lenny and Joe are sitting at Lenny's table having a coffee.

>   JOE
>   Seriously, I must have applied to
>   fifty jobs already and not a single
>   offer.

                                        (CONTINUED)

CONTINUED:

                    LENNY
          Maybe it's just that you are applying
          for the wrong kind of job for your
          skill-set?

                    JOE
          Are you kidding me, Lenny? I think I
          applied for EVERY type of job out
          there. You name it! I just wish that
          drumming was a normal-paying day-job.
          I'd already be hired.

Lenny abruptly jumps out of his seat.

                    LENNY
          Oh NO! I completely forgot that I
          have Mike Botts from the band 'Bread'
          meeting me at the studio this
          morning. I hired him to lay some drum
          tracks down. I should have been there
          by now! I'd give you a ride to your
          apartment but the studio is the
          opposite way. Take your time to
          finish your coffee and let yourself
          out, if you don't mind.

Lenny grabs his keys off the counter and runs out the door.
Joe puts his head in his hands for a moment, then gets up
with his coffee, pours it down the drain and heads out the
door, closing it in frustration.

                                        CUT TO:

EXT. COLDWATER CANYON BOULEVARD - MOMENTS LATER

Joe is walking down the sidewalk. Eventually, he picks up
the pace to a fast walk, then a jog, then an all-out run for
several blocks until he reaches his apartment complex.

                                        CUT TO:

INT. JOE AND JEFF'S APARTMENT - MOMENTS LATER

Frantically, Joe is unpacking the drum boxes that are in his
apartment hallway, and setting up his drum-set in the middle
of the living room. Once set up, Joe sits behind the drums
and breaks into a major drum solo. After a minute or so, he
stops to adjust a cymbal stand and hears knocking at the
door. He answers it to find an attractive female in the
apartment building hallway.

                                        (CONTINUED)

CONTINUED:

DIANE, Attractive and conservatively dressed

>   DIANE
>   Hi there. I'm Diane, one of your
>   neighbors.

>   JOE
>   Oh... Hey, I'm Joe. I'm sorry for all
>   the noise. I'll stop playing.

>   DIANE
>   No... Don't get me wrong. I thought
>   you sounded great. I'm a drummer
>   myself, but if the building manager
>   was home she'd probably kick you out
>   of here. Come check this out.

Joe follows Diane down the hall to her apartment on the
opposite side of the building's courtyard.

>   CUT TO:

INT. DIANE'S LIVING ROOM - MOMENTS LATER

A drum-set is assembled in the middle of the room. There are
acoustic guitars scattered about, as well as music stands.

>   DIANE
>   Check this out, Joe.

Diane sits down at the drums and plays an amazing drum solo
of her own, yet the volume of the drums and cymbals is
extremely low. She finishes her brief solo then signals for
Joe to come around to her side of the drums, exposing black
rubber pads on each drum head and cymbal top.

>   DIANE (cont'd)
>   These are new drum pads that just
>   came out. I love them because I don't
>   need to rent a studio any more. I
>   even give drum lessons right here and
>   my neighbors have no idea that I am.

>   JOE
>   Those are awesome. YOU are awesome.
>   I'm guessing you've been drumming for
>   a long time?

>   DIANE
>   Yeah... Maybe too long, but it is all
>   I know. Both my husband and I are
>   studio musicians.
>   (MORE)

>   (CONTINUED)

CONTINUED:

                         DIANE (cont'd)
              He's a bassist, and in the studio as
              we speak, thankfully. With all of the
              new synthesizers and drum-machines
              coming out, everyone is fighting for
              less studio jobs these days.

                         JOE
              Is that a hard part of the business
              to break into?

                         DIANE
              It is all about who you know. Of
              course, the talent needs to be there,
              but if you aren't connected it is
              nearly impossible. We've been out
              here for 12 years now. My husband
              tours with Air Supply, and when he's
              not on tour he grabs what little
              studio bass work he can get. Today,
              he is laying the bass track for a new
              McDonald's commercial. You just
              getting into town?

                         JOE
              Yeah, I'm here from Rhode Island.
              Came out for a job that has fallen
              through.

                         DIANE
              Ooh... That is tough. Well all I can
              say is network the heck out of
              yourself and the studio work may
              start to trickle-in within a year or
              so.

                         JOE
              A year?

                         DIANE
              Tough business. You sound great, so
              hang in there.

                                        CUT TO:

INT. JOE AND JEFF'S APARTMENT - MOMENTS LATER

Joe is on the phone with Steven at Married with Children.

                                        (CONTINUED)

CONTINUED:

> JOE
> Hey Steven... I really hate putting
> you on the spot like this, and it is
> OK if you say no, but is there any
> way that you could get me an
> interview with the hiring manager at
> 'Married... with Children'? Things
> kind-of fell through and I'm
> beginning to panic a bit.

FADE TO:

INT. MARRIED WITH CHILDREN MANAGEMENT OFFICE - NEXT MORNING

Joe is being interviewed by a man in a suit who is sitting
behind a desk. It is toward the end of the interview.

MANAGER, Middle-aged man, partly bald and wearing glasses at
the end of his nose.

> MANAGER
> Well, you haven't been in town very
> long. How is it that I may be certain
> that you will be staying in Los
> Angeles long-term if I were to hire
> you?

Joe adjusts his body to the edge of his seat.

> JOE
> Sir, I've been coming out to L.A.
> several times each year for the
> better part of a decade now. This is
> like my second home. I love it here,
> and this job will finally give me the
> means to stay here permanently.

The Manager stands up and extends his hand to shake Joe's.

> MANAGER
> Welcome on board. Call me when you
> get a car, registered and insured in
> your name, as you are going to need
> it for your new job here on the
> studio lot.

FADE TO:

INT. JOE AND JEFF'S APARTMENT - LATER THAT DAY

Joe is on the telephone with Lenny.

(CONTINUED)

CONTINUED:

                         JOE
          Yes, I'm very excited about the job.
          The only thing is that I need a car,
          registered and insured in my name
          before I can begin. You had mentioned
          being willing to give your old car to
          me if I moved out here. I really hate
          asking, but is that offer still on
          the table?

                         LENNY
                    (off screen)
          I have both good and bad news
          regarding the car. The bad news is
          that I sold the car for four-hundred
          dollars a few months ago. The good
          news is that they never came to pick
          it up, so if you have four-hundred
          bucks that we can give back to them,
          the car is yours.

                         JOE
          Deal. I will go to the bank tomorrow
          and withdraw the money.

                         LENNY
                    (off screen)
          OK, but I should make you aware that
          the car needs some extensive
          electrical work done to it before it
          will start, so you'll need to tow it
          to a garage that specializes in that
          type of auto work.

                         JOE
          Any idea how much that'll cost?

                         LENNY
                    (off screen)
          My guess would be two, three-hundred
          bucks?

                         JOE
          I could probably swing that. Let me
          start making some calls to get a tow-
          truck hired for tomorrow.

                                        FADE TO:

INT. AUTOMOTIVE MECHANIC SHOP - EARLY AFTERNOON

Joe is pacing in the customer waiting area while his "new" car is being worked on. The late-model Mazda RX7 can be seen through the large window that looks into the auto-stall area. The mechanic closes the hood and starts the car up. He walks in and works up an invoice.

MECHANIC 1, Middle-age man wearing a full-body jump-suit, with grease on his fingers and face

                    MECHANIC 1
          So we got her up and running for ya.
          The damage will be three-hundred and
          forty-seven.

He hands Joe an invoice with greasy finger prints on it.

                    MECHANIC 1 (cont'd)
          You realize that you'll need new
          tires all-around for that puppy to
          pass inspection, right?

                    JOE
               (handing the mechanic
                a stack of bills)
          Ugh! Really? I sure wasn't planning
          on that. Can you tell me where I can
          buy inexpensive tires?

The mechanic writes an address on a greasy envelope, and hands it back to Joe, along with seven dollars.

                    MECHANIC 1
          Here... These guys will set you up
          for little dough.

                    JOE
               (looking at the seven
                dollars)
          I thought I counted out the exact
          amount?

                    MECHANIC 1
          You look like you need a break today.
          I rounded it down to Three-Forty.

                    JOE
          Thanks, man. I'll take any break I
          can get at this point.

                                             CUT TO:

INT. JOE'S CAR - MOMENTS LATER

Joe is showing concern on his face while driving his car to
the next mechanic shop, as a constant loud percussive
banging is coming up from under the floor between the driver
and passenger seats. We see the car pull in and park in
front of one of the garage doors. Joe walks through the
customer entrance door and up the the counter.

SERVICE CLERK, White button-down shirt with a patch of the
name 'Baldy's Tires' sewn to it.

                    SERVICE CLERK
          How can we help you today?

                    JOE
          I have a late-model RX-7 that I need
          tires for. Can you put on the least
          expensive tires that you've got?

                    SERVICE CLERK
          Can do...

The clerk begins typing into a computer.

                    JOE
          Also, do you folks do mechanical work
          in addition to tires?

                    SERVICE CLERK
          We do it all, my man.

                    JOE
          Then, once the tires are installed,
          can a mechanic take the car for a
          spin? There is a loud banging noise
          coming from underneath the car and
          I'd like to know what it is.

                    SERVICE CLERK
          You've got it. Give us a half-hour.

                                        CUT TO:

EXT. BALDY'S TIRES PARKING LOT - (ONE HOUR LATER)

The mechanic is pulling back into the parking lot after
taking it for a spin. Joe meets him as soon as he gets out
of the car. The mechanic is shaking his head.

                    JOE
          That good, huh?

                                        (CONTINUED)

CONTINUED:

MECHANIC 2, Wearing the same jump-suit as the mechanic from
the first auto mechanic shop, and looking like he could be
the first mechanic's brother, though completely bald.

                    MECHANIC 2
          Son? Sounds to me like you need a new
          universal joint.

                    JOE
          And that sounds to me like it's going
          to be expensive.

                    MECHANIC 2
          I'll need to price it out, but with
          labor and all, I'm guessing that
          you're looking at about five-hundred
          bucks.

                    JOE
          Damned!

Joe kicks one of the tires.

                    JOE (cont'd)
          Oh, I'm sorry... I know that you just
          installed that tire. It's just that
          I'm running out of money really
          quickly. I'll need to go back to my
          bank tomorrow morning. Will it be
          safe for me to drive the car back to
          Studio City for the night, then drive
          it back here in the morning the way
          the car is?

                    MECHANIC 2
          Well, you run the risk that it'll let
          go but it might be fine.

The mechanic takes a greasy business card out of his jump-
suit.

                    MECHANIC 2 (cont'd)
          If it does break down, here is the
          number to call for a tow.

Joe looks at the business card and notices that it is for
the same garage that he had the car's electrical work done
at.

                    JOE
          Right. Wish me luck.

Joe gets into his car and drives away.

(CONTINUED)

CONTINUED:

FADE TO:

INT. JOE AND JEFF'S APARTMENT - MORNING (2 DAYS LATER)

The phone is ringing. Joe comes out of the bathroom with wet hair, wearing a towel and brushing his teeth. He wipes his mouth with a paper towel and answers the phone.

> JOE
> Hello?

> DONNY
> (off screen)
> Who else is doing what you're doing?

> JOE
> Hey, Man. Glad to hear your voice.

> DONNY
> (off screen)
> Yeah, I would've called earlier but got the sense that you were pissed at me and figured you'd reach out to me eventually, but I got tired of waiting. We all miss you back here.

> JOE
> Yeah? You and who else? I'm sure not Shelly.

> DONNY
> (off screen)
> I ran into Dave last night at The Fairway. He's pretty bummed out about you being away. He said that without The Threats he feels like a people without a nation.

> JOE
> I miss playing with those guys, too. Hey, I'm now employed by 'Married with Children'... Well, I will be starting Monday.

> DONNY
> (off screen)
> That's cool, but what happened to the job that Bibi was getting for you?

(CONTINUED)

CONTINUED:

                    JOE
Who knows? She went missing in
action. I'm excited about the Married
gig, though I need to jump through
hoops to actually start. Needed a car
registered and insured in my name, so
I finally got a car, then a gazillion
things fixed on it, which has eaten
away at a big chunk of my savings.
Good thing I start work on Monday. I
just need to get it inspected today
'cause they won't register it without
proof of inspection. After that I am
good to go.

                    DONNY
                 (off screen)
Good for you, Bud. Hey, I got your
address from your Mom last week and
mailed some beer money out your way,
seeing as we didn't get a chance to
have that going away beer when you
were leaving. There might be a little
extra in that check to help with a
bill or two also.

                    JOE
Dude, you didn't have to do that, but
if there is ever a time that I'd
accept it, it is now. Thanks so much,
Donny.

                                        CUT TO:

EXT. APARTMENT PARKING GARAGE - LATE MORNING

Joe checks his mail box and extracts three envelopes. Two
are addressed for him, and one for Jeff. He gets into his
car, starts it up, and opens his mail before backing out of
his parking spot. One envelope includes a check from Donny,
and the other one includes a card and a check from Joe's
mother.

Backing his car out of the space, Joe gets to the street and
he turns his left directional light on. In his side-view
mirror, he notices a wet gleam reflecting his signal light,
shining up from the pavement where his car was parked. He
gets out of the car to check it out and notices a puddle of
transmission fluid.

                    JOE
Are you freakin' kidding me?!

                                      (CONTINUED)

CONTINUED:

Joe gets back in his car and he turns the right directional
light on instead, and pulls out onto the street.

                                              CUT TO:

EXT. VENTURA BOULEVARD CAR WASH - MOMENTS LATER

Joe is standing off to the side while a few car wash workers
are pre-soaking his car before they take it through the
automated wash station. One of the workers walks up to Joe.

CAR WASH WORKER, Early twenties, Mexican descent, wearing
baggy jeans and a muscle shirt

                    CAR WASH WORKER
          Hey Man, any interest in selling your
          car?

                    JOE
          No, I need it for my job.

                    CAR WASH WORKER
          You sure, Man? I'll give you cash
          money for it.

                    JOE
          I wish I could, but I need it. You
          guys wash the undercarriage, too,
          right?

                    CAR WASH WORKER
          Every part of that car is gonna
          shine... Top, Bottom, Front, Back...

                                              CUT TO:

EXT. AUTOMOBILE INSPECTION STATION - MOMENTS LATER

Joe is leaning on a fence, looking at his car hooked-up to
several inspection apparatus in an open car stall. The
Inspection Worker walks up to him.

INSPECTION WORKER, Middle-aged man wearing a blue jump-suit

                    INSPECTION WORKER
          The emissions test is reading high.
          Usually I can tweak a few things to
          help it to pass, but I'll need a good
          half-hour or so. There's coffee
          inside if you'd like a cup.

                                              (CONTINUED)

CONTINUED:

                    JOE
          Thanks, but I'll take a walk to the
          bank across the street. Whatever you
          can do to make it pass will be most
          appreciated, sir.

                                        CUT TO:

INT. BANK TELLER WINDOW - MOMENTS LATER

Joe is trying to get the two checks cashed that were mailed
to him by his mother and Donny.

BANK TELLER, Heavy-set woman in her early 50's, wearing a
pant-suit, and a pin on her lapel that says 'Smile, I'm
Brenda'

                    BANK TELLER
          I'm sorry, but I can only cash the
          check for fifty dollars. You don't
          have enough in your account to cover
          the two-hundred and fifty dollar
          check, unfortunately.

                    JOE
          It's Brenda?

The Bank Teller nods.

                    JOE (cont'd)
          Brenda, what if you process the check
          and I'll come back in a few days for
          the cash once it clears?

                    BANK TELLER
          I'm sorry. It doesn't quite work like
          that.

                    JOE
          Well, then, how CAN we make this
          work?

                    BANK TELLER
          The only way is to have the funds
          already in your account to cover the
          check.

                    JOE
          Well, what do poor people do when
          they need to cash a check, Brenda?

                                        (CONTINUED)

CONTINUED:

                         BANK TELLER
              Well, they don't usually come in
              here.

                         JOE
              Yeah, well one did today, Brenda.

                         BANK TELLER
              You sure read the name on my pin
              correctly, but that look on your face
              tells me you skipped the word SMILE.

                         JOE
              You can keep the smile. I'll just
              take my check back, and the fifty
              from the check that you CAN cash.

                                        CUT TO:

EXT. AUTOMOBILE INSPECTION STATION - MOMENTS LATER

The inspection worker is handing Joe his car keys, and
showing him a report print-out.

                         INSPECTION WORKER
              I really tried everything I could,
              but as you can see, your car is WAY
              over what the State of California
              allows for auto emissions.

                         JOE
              Is there anything at all you can do?
              ANYTHING? You have no idea how
              important it is for me to get this
              car registered.

                         INSPECTION WORKER
              This car would take a lot of work to
              get it to where it needs to be.
              Considering the age and condition of
              the automobile, I don't think it
              would make sense to put that kind of
              money into it. I'll tell you what, I
              won't charge you for the time that we
              spent on it today.

Joe tries to speak, but can barely get a word out. He starts
up the car and drives away in shock.

                                        CUT TO:

INT. JOE AND JEFF'S APARTMENT - MOMENTS LATER

Joe walks into his living room, looking drained and
deflated. He is carrying his mail from earlier in the day.
He places the envelope addressed to Jeff on the kitchen
counter, along with the $250 check from Donny and the $50
from the check that he was able to cash. He carries the card
from his mother, and walks over to the living room area, and
sits on top of one of the few boxes from the move to L.A.
that is still unopened and on the floor. The box has the
words 'Joe's Sentimental Stuff' written in black marker on
the side of it. Joe leans back against the wall and re-reads
the card from his Mom.

"Dear Joe,
I was crying too hard on the day that you left, so I
couldn't get the words out that I wanted to say to you. I
remember how, when you were feeling down as a child, I could
always make you feel better by telling you that you were
very special to me because you were my only boy. If only I
could have made you feel better with those words in the wake
of your break-up with Shelly. I know how your heart has been
hurting, and I hope that you do find much healing and
success in Los Angeles. You are extremely talented and you
will go as far as you want to take your dreams... and please
don't EVER forget that you are VERY special.
Love you,
Mom"

Joe wipes a tear from his eye, as he gets up and begins
pacing around the room with his mother's card in his hand.
He talks to himself out loud.

                    JOE
          Special... Yeah, so special that I
          can't seem to get anywhere in L.A....
          or in life... How special can I
          be?... Follow my dreams... yeah,
          right into the ground... Who the hell
          cares about my dream?... Who the hell
          cares about me?... Obviously, not the
          one who said that she'll be with me
          for our entire lives... The one who
          said she believed in me and my
          dream...

Joe places the card from his mother on the counter near the
check from Don and the mail for Jeff, and then grabs the
garbage can and brings it over to the box labeled
"sentimental", and tears open the top of the box.

(CONTINUED)

CONTINUED:

                    JOE (cont'd)
    ...The one who wrote me a freaking
    box worth of cards about how much she
    loved me... What freaking bull-shit!!

Extracting card after card from the box... Joe is ripping
them in half, reading a few along the way, and throwing them
into the garbage can bag in an angry frenzy. He gets to some
promotional posters of The Threats, tearing those in half,
too.

                    JOE (cont'd)
    So much for dreams... Then you wake
    up and find yourself nowhere!

Joe comes across the newspaper that the post-office worker
gave to him, that includes the photo and story of The
Threats performing a benefit concert, and tosses it into the
garbage.

                    JOE (cont'd)
    Of course... Help others... Do good
    in the world and it will come back to
    you... Right!

Joe ties up the garbage bag and heads to the building's
garbage chute, throwing the bag into it.

                    JOE (cont'd)
    Goodbye Shelly... Goodbye Dream...

He returns to his apartment living room, sits on the floor
in tears, and turns the television on. There is an
inspirational speaker on the screen, talking to a studio
audience.

                INSPIRATIONAL SPEAKER
          (coming through TV
          speaker)
    If you want to move ahead or achieve
    that something that you truly desire,
    you must get rid of the negative
    thoughts of "I can't - I won't - I'm
    not good enough", and replace those
    words with "I can - I will - I am
    better than good!"... Then, write
    down what it is that you desire and
    envision it as it relates to you...
    If you want a new job, picture
    yourself actually doing it and write
    down your thoughts...
                (MORE)

CONTINUED:

                    INSPIRATIONAL SPEAKER (cont'd)
          If you desire love, imagine what it
          would feel like if you finally found
          that perfect partner, and write it
          down...

Joe turns off the television, walks into Jeff's bedroom,
turns on his keyboard and begins to play some chords while
humming a melody. He finds a pad and a pen and begins to
write...

"You walked into my room - undressed my doubts -
Now I believe that a heroine pulls a drowning man from the
sea of doom to a fairy-tale - I do
In a windy past my sail would tear on nights without a moon
You're the first light of a dawning
Come show me afternoon
If you let me go in a thousand years - No - Don't
For that's too soon
Two hearts make one evolving - and I think it's true
Eternal love - I do
If I was acting the play of Cupid, I'd forget my part
Or wore a mask like Halloween
Wouldn't I be talking to ghosts?
I can see that you're not
I would pray for love when I felt my heart
Was an empty tomb - Then you appear just like an Angel..."

Joe struggles with figuring out what the last few lines
should be. He writes a few words down and scribbles over
them... does that a few times, then rips the paper out of
the notebook and puts it in his pocket. He then goes into
his bathroom and removes a hoop ear-ring from his left ear,
and replaces it with a dangling cross.

                         JOE
                  (speaking to himself)
          I need a change of scenery. I'm not
          gonna find my perfect partner by
          sitting in here by myself.

Grabbing the $50 from the kitchen counter, Joe walks out of
his apartment.

                                                  CUT TO:

INT. CASA VEGA MEXICAN RESTAURANT - EVENING

Joe is sitting at the bar. There is a Margarita drink in
front of him, as well as the sheet of lyrics that he was
working on earlier. We see Joe twirling a pen between two
fingers as he stares at the sheet in deep thought.

                                              (CONTINUED)

CONTINUED:

He glances over at the dining area where he and Shelly enjoyed their engagement dinner, shaking his head in disappointment while yawning. He then scans the bar area and notices an attractive woman sitting in a corner booth, also yawning, and looking at Joe. He turns back toward his lyric sheet, then back again at the woman. This time the woman gives a small wave to Joe, and he replies with a nod, while noticing that she is writing something, too. Joe returns to his lyric sheet and takes a sip from his drink. The woman sits on the stool next to Joe.

JUNE, Attractive mid-30's woman, elegantly dressed.

                    JUNE
          Is this seat available?

Joe, being taken off-guard, swallows his sip, places his glass down, and flips his lyric sheet over.

                    JOE
          By all means, it is yours.

                    JUNE
          I've been noticing that you're a
          writer?

                    JOE
          Usually, but it seems like I have
          writer's block for the last verse of
          this song.

                    JUNE
          Ah, a song-writer. I'm a writer
          myself... a novel-writer. My name is
          June.

The two shake hands.

                    JOE
          Nice to meet you. I'm Joe. Wow, a
          novel-writer. Have you been doing
          that for a while?

                    JUNE
          I suppose you could say that. Many
          people who read novels would be
          familiar with me.

                    JOE
          That's really cool. Admittedly, I
          haven't read many novels. Been mostly
          all about the music for me.

CONTINUED:

> JUNE
> How refreshing. Someone who doesn't know who I am. Do you like to play darts?

> JOE
> Actually, yes. My best friend in New England has a dart board. We'd play all the time.

> JUNE
> New England, huh? I was trying to figure out your accent. Well, I'm done writing for today, and I'm guessing that you are, too. Let me take you to a hole-in-the-wall where they have the best dartboards.

> JOE
> Thanks, but I don't have a ton of money right now.

> JUNE
> My treat. Come-on, it's just on the other side of the Valley. You might want to get your car out of valet and park it on the street in-case we get back late.

> JOE
> I actually walked here. OK, sounds like fun, but at least allow me to buy the first drink.

CUT TO:

INT. DIVE BAR - 20 MINUTES LATER

Joe is standing at the bar, ordering two drinks. He watches June as she heads to the back of the bar and has some sort of financial exchange with a burly man. Joe gives a puzzling look as he turns back to the bar to pay for the drinks. June returns to the bar.

> JUNE
> So, you ready to get your butt kicked at darts?

> JOE
> Bring it on.

(CONTINUED)

CONTINUED:

June signals to the bartender...

                    JUNE
          Two shots of Jagermeister!

                    JOE
          I actually don't do shots. I
          typically stick with beer.

                    JUNE
          Awww, come-on... One ain't going to
          hurt you.

We see a sequence of June and Joe taking turns throwing
darts at the dartboard, and a waitress returning several
times with more shots of Jagermeister throughout the
sequence.

                    JOE
               (slurring)
          Well, that's four games in a row that
          you've won. I'm done.

                    JUNE
          Let's get out of here.

                                        CUT TO:

INT. JUNE'S CAR - MOMENTS LATER

Joe is looking visibly intoxicated in this scene, then a
cut-to the double-vision that Joe is seeing through his eyes
from the passenger seat while June drives.

                    JUNE
          So, why the hell do you have that
          hanging from your ear?

Joe feels his ear to remember what may be hanging.

                    JOE
               (slurring)
          Oh, this is a cross.

                    JUNE
          I know what it is. You don't actually
          believe in that crap do you?

                    JOE
          Christianity? I do. Why? You don't?

                                        (CONTINUED)

CONTINUED:

                    JUNE
          It's a bunch of bull.

As June begins to rub his thigh, Joe is trying to focus on
their location as much as he can, and realizes that they are
approaching the closest intersection to his apartment. The
car stops at the red light.

                    JOE
              (slurring)
          Well, this is close to my place, so
          I'll just get out here. Nice to meet
          you.

                    JUNE
          What? Don't you want me to come in?

                    JOE
              (slurring)
          I'm exhausted. Thanks for driving.

Joe gets out of the car and stumbles his way behind an
apartment complex that isn't his. He waits for the light to
change and for June's car to pull away before he crosses the
street toward his actual apartment building.

                                        CUT TO:

INT. JOE'S BATHROOM - MOMENTS LATER

Joe is on the floor, leaning into the toilet bowl and
vomiting.

We then see Joe asleep on the bathroom floor and a time-
lapse of the room getting brighter as the morning sun rises.
Joe wakes up with apparent signs of a hangover (headache and
slow movement). He slowly gets up, showers and brushes his
teeth. He walks over to the keyboard in George's bedroom.
Joe pulls out the lyric sheet from within his pocket and
proceeds to write the last line of the song down.

"Do you believe in God when you see miracles?
In you - I do"

Joe then tries the entire song.

<PLAY SONG 'I DO'>

                                        (CONTINUED)

CONTINUED:

Jeff comes home and walks into the room as Joe is playing.

> JEFF
> Hey!

> JOE
> (startled)
> Oh, Hey... I haven't seen you in
> forever.

Jeff walks over and turns the keyboard off.

> JEFF
> I thought I told you not to play this
> when I'm not here.

> JOE
> Well, when the heck WOULD I get to
> play it? You're NEVER here. I had a
> song idea... Big deal.

> JEFF
> You land a job yet?

> JOE
> That's a long story.

Joe follows Jeff as he walks into the kitchen and begins to
look in the cupboards and refrigerator for food.

> JOE (cont'd)
> You won't find much in there.

Joe grabs the envelope addressed to Jeff that is on the
counter and hands it to him.

> JOE (cont'd)
> This came in for you.

Jeff opens it.

> JEFF
> Oh, good. It's a check from my
> father.

> JOE
> Great. When you go to cash it, would
> you mind cashing a check that Donny
> sent to me? The bank told me that I
> didn't have enough in my account to
> cover it.

CONTINUED:

                    JEFF
        I don't really need to cash mine
        right away, so I won't be going to
        the bank.

                    JOE
        Well, would you mind going anyway so
        I can get mine cashed? I'm really
        hurting for some cash right now.

                    JEFF
        No, I've got to do some laundry then
        re-pack the SUV. I'm heading up to
        San Francisco this afternoon to visit
        with a friend for a while. I'll most-
        likely spend Christmas there.

                    JOE
        Dude, seriously?

                    JEFF
        What do you want me to tell you? I've
        made some plans.

                    JOE
        You can tell me that you'll help to
        get my check cashed so I can freaking
        survive.

                    JEFF
        Sorry, man. I'm sure that you'll
        figure it out. You always do.

                    JOE
        Wow... Thanks a lot. Merry Christmas
        to you, too.

Joe leaves the apartment, slamming the door on the way out.

                                     CUT TO:

EXT. MINI-MART GAS STATION NEXT TO APARTMENT - MOMENTS LATER

Joe walks by a homeless man on the way into the store. The
man's face is covered by a newspaper that he is reading. Joe
focuses on the hand-written cardboard sign that leans
against an old shopping cart, which reads "Homeless but not
hopeless. Willing to work for food or money". A moment
later, we see Joe exit the store, holding a hot dog that he
purchased, as he slips the change into his pocket while
passing the homeless man.

                                    (CONTINUED)

CONTINUED:

Joe heads down the street for a walk, as the homeless man folds up the paper and places it in the shopping cart with his other possessions.

DISSOLVE TO:

INT. JOE AND JEFF'S APARTMENT - EARLY EVENING

Joe returns from his walk to his dark apartment. He flips a few light-switches on and notices that Jeff's keyboard is no longer set-up in his room. He shakes his head with disappointment and heads back to the kitchen and empties his pocket next to the un-cashed check. He counts out six-dollars and thirty-seven cents, and begins to pace around his apartment. He is nervously wringing his hands while panicking and shaking his head. He eventually puts the money back into his pocket and exits the apartment.

CUT TO:

EXT. COLDWATER CANYON BOULEVARD - MOMENTS LATER

Joe is walking down the sidewalk and he pauses to listen to some Christmas carolers that are gathered in a doorway. They are singing a holiday classic.

                    CHRISTMAS CAROLERS
          For we need a little Christmas -
          Right this very minute - Candles in
          the window - Carols at the spinet -
          And we need a little Christmas -
          Right this very minute - We need a
          little Christmas now

Joe continues walking, while talking to himself.

                    JOE
          No kidding. I could use a little...
          No... I could use a LOT of Christmas
          right about now.

Joe walks up to a small church nestled between large apartment buildings. It is the size of a small bungalow. Joe reads the sign outside the church, which says 'Little Brown Church - All are welcome - Come in and pray'.

CUT TO:

INT. LITTLE BROWN CHURCH - MOMENTS LATER

As he surveys the interior of the small church, Joe sits in one of the few pews. He looks up at the painting of Jesus that is hanging above the altar, then hangs his head and prays with all of his spiritual might.

                    JOE
              (speaking low, but
              audibly)
          Dear God... PLEASE... I need you to
          hear me tonight. Please give me
          direction. Please give me a sign so I
          can definitively know what it is that
          I need to do. I'm running out of time
          because I'm running out of money...
          Should that come between a person and
          his dream? PLEASE God...
          Our Father who art in Heaven,
          hallowed be thy name.
          Thy kingdom come.
          Thy will be done
          on earth as it is in Heaven.
          Give us this day our daily bread,
          and forgive us our trespasses,
          as we forgive those who trespass
          against us,
          and lead us not into temptation,
          but deliver us from evil.

He then injects some of the lyrics from the Christmas carol he heard being sung on the way to the small church.

                    JOE (cont'd)
          For I've grown a little leaner...
          I've grown a little colder... I've
          grown a little sadder... I've grown a
          little older... and I need a little
          Angel sitting on my shoulder... I
          need a little Christmas now.

Joe stands up and nods at the painting of Jesus. He notices that Jesus' eyes appear to be following him as he exits the pew, and shrugs-off an apparent chill up his spine.

                                        CUT TO:

EXT. MINI-MART GAS STATION NEXT TO APARTMENT - MOMENTS LATER

Walking into the mini-mart, Joe passes the same homeless man that he passed earlier in the day.

INT. MINI-MART

Checking out the prices of single-wrapped burritos in the frozen section, Joe decides on one and brings it to the cashier. After paying for it he counts the amount of money that he has left to his name. Two-dollars and change...

                    JOE
          (speaking to himself)
     Well... This is it...

He walks out of the store and hands the two dollars to the homeless man and continues walking toward his apartment next door.

ONE EYE DON, Homeless man dressed in ragged clothes.

                    ONE EYE DON
     Thanks a lot, Joe!

Joe turns around to see if it is him that the homeless man is talking to. He notices that one of his eyes is completely white and smaller than the other as the homeless man looks into Joe's eyes.

                    JOE
     How do you know my name?

The homeless man reaches into the shopping cart that holds his possessions and pulls out the copy of the Rhode Island newspaper that Joe threw away the day before while getting rid of his sentimental things. The man opens it up to the photo of Joe's band that accompanied the article about the benefit show that he performed, and points Joe out in the picture.

                    ONE EYE DON
     This is you, right?

                    JOE
     Yes, but how did you get that paper?

                    ONE EYE DON
     When a person lives on the streets,
     they sometimes need to go through
     other people's trash to survive. You
     live in that building right there,
     correct?

                    JOE
     Yeah, but why would you pull that
     paper out of my trash and keep it?

(CONTINUED)

CONTINUED:

                    ONE EYE DON
          Because it reminded me of when I was
          a child. I used to live in
          Massachusetts on the border of Rhode
          Island.

                    JOE
          What brought you out to Los Angeles?

                    ONE EYE DON
          Well, it's kind-of a long story, but
          my mother died when I was four years
          old. By the time I was seven, I was
          placed into an orphanage because my
          father had punished me by splashing
          acid into one of my eyes. I ran away
          from that orphanage when I was
          sixteen and ended up here in
          California, where I went to work as a
          roofer. Eventually, I saved up enough
          money to buy my own truck and
          equipment and began to work for
          myself. Things were going pretty well
          until my truck was stolen, along with
          all of the equipment that was in it.
          With no insurance, not much money
          saved, and no family to lean on for
          help, I quickly found myself
          homeless.

                    JOE
          Wow... Where do you sleep?

                    ONE EYE DON
          In an abandoned house with my
          girlfriend. I come out here to try
          and get enough money for us to eat
          each day, then I put the rest aside
          so I may buy another truck and
          equipment to get back to work.

                    JOE
          I admire you.

                    ONE EYE DON
          What is your story?

                    JOE
          I'm in a tough place, but it pales in
          comparison to all that you have been
          through.

CONTINUED:

                        ONE EYE DON
        Well, that doesn't make it, or you,
        any less important. What is going on
        in your life?

                        JOE
        As you know from the newspaper, I am
        a musician and songwriter. Since the
        age of fourteen I have been
        performing in nightclubs and
        theaters, and have always been told
        to follow my dreams. That if I worked
        hard enough, I'd achieve them. One of
        my dreams is to land a record deal so
        my songs can be heard everywhere,
        which is why I came out here.
        Unfortunately, the job that I thought
        was waiting for me fell through.
        Another job opened up for me but I
        needed a car for it. I ended up
        buying one and sinking the rest of my
        money into fixing it, only to learn
        that I can't register it because it
        fails the California emissions test.
        I am now out of money and not sure
        what to do. If I return to Rhode
        Island too soon I'd feel like such a
        failure. What would my family and
        friends think of me?

                        ONE EYE DON
        It's actually quite simple, Joe. You
        have family and friends back home
        that you can lean on. Go back there
        and re-group. You can always return
        to L.A., but if you stay here now you
        will certainly become homeless like
        me.

                        JOE
        Hmm. I'm going to consider that.

                        ONE EYE DON
        Is there another reason why you came
        out here?

                        JOE
        I don't know... Maybe. I was engaged
        to a girl but she broke it off. It
        was difficult for me to see her
        around town with another guy.

CONTINUED:

                ONE EYE DON
      Would that be Shelly?

                JOE
      How would you know about Shelly?

                ONE EYE DON
      Maybe by the hundred or so cards from
      her that you threw away.

He reaches into his shopping cart once again and holds up
one of the cards.

                ONE EYE DON (cont'd)
      I really like the picture on the
      front of this card, and thought I'd
      bring it back to my girlfriend and
      hang it on the wall. Hey, let me give
      you your money back, considering the
      tough spot that you are in.

Joe notices some writing from Shelly on the back side of the
card.

                JOE
      Actually, do you mind if I just take
      the card back? It's kind-of personal.

                ONE EYE DON
      Of course not. Here, my friend.

                JOE
      Thanks... and thanks for our chat. I
      really needed that tonight.

Joe extends his hand and the two shake.

                JOE (cont'd)
      I guess I'll head in. What is your
      name?

                ONE EYE DON
      You can call me 'One Eye Don'. That's
      how I'm known around here.

                JOE
      I'll see you again, One Eye Don.

Tears begin to stream down Joe's face as he walks toward his
apartment building.

                FADE TO:

INT. COLUMBIA BAR & GRILL - EVENING

The 'Married with Children' Christmas party is underway, and
Joe is sitting at a booth with singer/songwriter/actress,
Nancy Priddy, and her daughter Christina Applegate.

                    JOE
          So, considering everything that has
          happened over the past several
          months, and everything that did NOT
          happen, I now think that it is time
          for me to go back to the East Coast
          and regroup. Believe it or not, I met
          a homeless man last night that put
          everything into perspective for me.
          It will be most difficult for me to
          pursue and achieve my musical dreams
          while living on the streets, which is
          most-likely what will happen if I
          stay here.

NANCY, A very attractive and well-dressed middle-aged woman

                    NANCY
          I'll tell you what, Joe... Do
          yourself a favor. When you get back
          to Rhode Island, MAKE your musical
          dreams come true, and record your OWN
          CD. Don't wait for the greedy jerks
          in the music industry to sign you.
          Sign yourself... Go into the
          recording studio and release all of
          those great songs that you have
          bottled up inside of you so the rest
          of the world may hear your talent.
          You did all you could out here this
          time, so don't beat yourself up about
          having to leave. We'll miss you
          around here, but I have a feeling
          that your absence from Los Angeles
          will be temporary.

                    JOE
          Thanks, Nancy. I think that's just
          what I'll do. Regroup, record my own
          CD, and take it from there. I promise
          that I'll thank you, Christina, and
          the entire cast and crew of 'Married
          with Children' on the CD credits.
          You've all truly been my family away
          from home, and I'll miss you all.

(CONTINUED)

CONTINUED:

                    NANCY
          Well, you are still here right now,
          so let's go have some fun.

Nancy and Christina get up and lead Joe over to the dance
floor, joining several others already dancing and
celebrating the holidays.

                              DISSOLVE TO:

INT. JOE AND JEFF'S APARTMENT - EARLY AFTERNOON

Joe has the cordless phone between his ear and shoulder
while gathering articles, placing items into boxes, and
making a pile of his belongings in his living room.

                    JOE
          Jade, I'll be flying home in a few
          days, and plan on showing up at Mom's
          for the Christmas Eve party.

                    JADE
               (off screen)
          Wow... Well, it will be great to have
          you back, but are you sure about
          leaving Los Angeles?

                    JOE
          Honestly, I don't feel that I have a
          choice, considering the financial
          position that I'm in... But, that
          being said, I am feeling OK with my
          decision after spending some time
          with a homeless man who made me
          realize that I have many more
          opportunities back home than I do
          here. As a matter of fact, I am going
          to give him most of my belongings so
          he can eventually sell them and put
          the money toward his dream of buying
          a pick-up truck and getting back to
          work. I'll keep my clothes and
          guitar, and ship my drums back to
          Rhode Island.

                    JADE
               (off screen)
          Do you need some money to ship your
          drums back?

                                        (CONTINUED)

CONTINUED:

                    JOE
          Thanks, Jade, but I should be OK. I
          sold my car to a guy that works at
          the car wash down the street. He said
          that he'll put some work into it to
          make it street legal again. He
          basically gave me the amount of money
          that I put into it, which will cover
          my shipping costs, food for the next
          few days, and transportation to the
          airport.

                    JADE
               (off screen)
          What about your apartment lease?

                    JOE
          My friend Bart from 'Married with
          Children' was looking for a new
          place, so he will be taking over my
          lease.

                    JADE
               (off screen)
          Well, it sounds like you have all of
          your bases covered. I can't wait to
          see you.

                    JOE
          Same here... Do me a favor and don't
          tell Mom that I'll be coming home. It
          will be fun to surprise her at the
          Christmas party.

                    JADE
               (off screen)
          That's a great idea. She has been
          missing you a lot. Hey, what if I
          rent a Santa Claus suit for you to
          wear, beard and all, and you can
          REALLY surprise Mom.

                    JOE
          Um, I'm not sure about wearing a
          Santa costume.

                    JADE
               (off screen)
          Awww... Come on... It'll be fun!

CONTINUED:

The door buzzer sounds...

                    JOE
          Hang on, Jade.

Joe presses the buzzer intercom.

                    JOE (cont'd)
          Who is it, please?

                    ONE EYE DON
                  (off screen)
          It's One Eye Don

                    JOE
          I'll buzz you in. Come on up to
          apartment 204.

Joe shifts his focus back to the phone conversation.

                    JOE (cont'd)
          Alright, Jade. I'll need to let you
          go. I'll see you on Christmas Eve.

                              DISSOLVE TO:

EXT. OUTSIDE JOE'S APARTMENT BUILDING - MOMENTS LATER

One Eye Don and Joe are packing the last of Joe's donations
into the back of a pick-up truck.

                    ONE EYE DON
          Are you sure about letting your
          television go to me, too? I mean,
          look at all this stuff that you are
          giving to me.

                    JOE
          It doesn't measure close to what you
          have given to me, my friend. I just
          truly hope that it helps to move you
          one step closer to buying that truck
          so you can get back to work. I can
          see the want, need, and hunger in
          your eye for that to happen.

                    ONE EYE DON
          Every last penny that comes from the
          sales of these material things will
          be going directly to my future pick-
          up truck. I can promise you that.

CONTINUED:

                    JOE
I'm so glad that you were able to
find this guy to pick up this load
today and bring it to the abandoned
house.

                 ONE EYE DON
Yeah, he pulls into the gas station
every day that I am out there and
buys me a coffee. If everyone was
this nice to me before I was
homeless, I may not have ever become
homeless. There are still very good
people in the world... like yourself,
Joe... which builds my hope of a
better tomorrow.

Joe pulls the card out of his pocket that he took back from
One Eye Don the night that they first met, and hands it to
him.

            ONE EYE DON (cont'd)
What's this?

                    JOE
I was thinking about it. There is no
reason for me to hang onto this card,
even though Shelly's handwriting is
on the back. I need to move on, and I
know how much you wanted to give it
to your girlfriend.

                 ONE EYE DON
I'll give one last bit of advice,
Joe. Forgive her. You won't be able
to truly heal or move on until you
do. I've forgiven everyone in my
past, including my father, and
whoever stole all of my equipment and
my pick-up truck. I have felt better
ever since... And, thanks for the
card. I will think of you every day
when I look at it, at which time I'll
say a prayer for you. I'll never
forget what you did for me here
today, and your good deed will come
back to you through God.

                    JOE
Thank you. I'll pray for you, too,
until the next time that we meet.
Always remember that I believe in
you.

                                      (CONTINUED)

CONTINUED:

The two hug. One Eye Don gets in the passenger side of the truck, and it pulls away. Joe watches it disappear and heads back into his empty apartment.

                                        FADE TO:

INT. JOE'S MOTHER'S HOUSE - CHRISTMAS EVE

Family is gathered to celebrate Christmas. Adults are hovering in the kitchen area, picking at food, drinking and conversing, while the younger family members are gathered in the living room as they try to guess what is in each wrapped package under the tree. A Santa Claus character (Joe) busts in through the front door, startling the revelers.

                    JOE
          HO-HO-HO!!

Joe walks up to his mother, who is staring at him and trying to figure out who just walked into her house behind the Santa beard.

                    JOE (cont'd)
          I'm HO-HO-HOME!

Joe reveals himself as he takes the beard off, causing his mother to burst into tears. They hug for a moment, and then Joe hugs all of the other relatives. He is handed a beer, and notices that the song he heard the carolers sing on the way to the Little Brown Church is playing on his mother's stereo.

"For we need a little music - We need a little laughter
We need a little singing ringing through the rafter
And we need a little snappy - Happy ever after
We need a little Christmas now"

Looking up and closing one eye, Joe mouths the words "Thank You"

                    JADE
          So, if you need a place to stay until
          you get your feet on the ground, Bill
          said that it would be OK for you to
          crash on our couch.

                    JOE
          That's really nice of you guys, but
          I've already accepted the same offer
          from Donny.
                    (MORE)

                                        (CONTINUED)

CONTINUED:
                          JOE (cont'd)
              It will be short-lived, as Randy
              offered me a job tending bar at the
              Living Room, which starts in a week,
              and I am supposed to check out a
              small apartment in Providence in a
              few days. It is only one room with a
              bathroom and kitchenette, but it is
              all that I'll need for a while. It is
              very inexpensive, and I want to save
              some money so I can go into the
              studio and record my own CD.

                          JADE
              Well, just know that the offer is
              always open if you change your mind
              or if anything falls through.

                          JOE
              You're the best, Jade.

The two hug.

                                         DISSOLVE TO:

INT. PROVIDENCE APARTMENT - MORNING

Joe and Donny are carrying boxes and following Joe's
landlord up a flight of stairs. The landlord opens the door
of one of his tenants' apartment on the way to Joe's small
space.

LANDLORD, Short, bald man in his sixties, wearing a suit but
looking disheveled

                          LANDLORD
              When the hell you gonna have my rent?

SARAH, Pretty girl in her mid-twenties

                          SARAH
              Get the hell out of here, you jerk!
              You can't just bust into my place
              like this!

Joe and Donny are just looking at each other with abrupt
concern.

                          LANDLORD
              Who's place is it? It is MY place!

                                              (CONTINUED)

CONTINUED:

                    SARAH
          Yeah? Well, the law says it is MY
          place right now. I'm a tenant with
          rights!

                    LANDLORD
          You're a pot-smoking hooker is what
          you are, and if you don't have my
          rent by next Friday, you'll be a
          homeless hooker!

The landlord slams the door, and continues down the hall as
if nothing happened.

                    LANDLORD (cont'd)
          Right this way, guys.

Joe, Donny, and the landlord enter Joe's new dwelling. It is
quite small, with a double bed, a chair, and not much room
to add too many additional things.

                    JOE
          I'll take it.

                    DONNY
               (under his breath)
          Are you crazy? This is a jail cell.

                    LANDLORD
          OK. Sign the lease and I own you for
          a year.

The landlord walks into the kitchenette and lays the lease
document on the counter for Joe to sign. Donny notices an
electrical extension cord draped over the sink faucet,
leading to the refrigerator.

                    DONNY
          Um... I'm pretty sure that an
          electrical cord running through the
          sink wouldn't meet code standards.

                    LANDLORD
          Oh... You're one of those, huh? Well,
          I'm glad I'm not renting the joint to
          you. Don't worry, it'll be re-routed
          in no time.

Joe signs the lease and the landlord hands him the keys.

                    LANDLORD (cont'd)
          Rent is due every other Friday. Don't
          fall behind.

CONTINUED:

The landlord exits. Joe takes bed sheets out of one of the boxes and begins to make the bed.

                    DONNY
          Dude, you are crazy. This place gives
          me the creeps.

                    JOE
          It's only temporary.

                    DONNY
          You just signed for a year.

                    JOE
          If I lived anywhere nicer I wouldn't
          be able to afford recording my own
          CD. That is my goal right now.

                    DONNY
          I still think you're crazy.

                              DISSOLVE TO:

Later that night, Joe is in bed, wakened by a mess of plaster and wetness covering his sheets and blanket that he is laying under.

                    JOE
          What the heck is THIS?

He gets up, turns on the lights, and sees that something leaked through the ceiling, causing a large chunk of plaster to crash down on top of his bed.

                    JOE (cont'd)
          Seriously? Ugh... Should have
          listened to Donny.

                              DISSOLVE TO:

INT. PROVIDENCE APARTMENT - LATE MORNING

Holding a bucket of ceiling plaster and a laundry basket with his laundered sheets, Joe climbs the stairs of his "new" apartment building. He notices the door to Sarah's apartment is wide open, with some wood debris sticking out into the hall. Looking in, Joe sees a hole in the wall and a broken chair scattered among other broken items on the floor, and he knocks on the open door. Sarah greets him with black mascara running down her cheeks, while slowly putting on and buttoning her shirt.

                                        (CONTINUED)

CONTINUED:

            JOE
Oh... I can come back. I just wanted
to make sure that you were OK.

           SARAH
No... It's cool. I appreciate it.
Just a really bad morning. My name is
Sarah.

            JOE
I'm Joe. Do you mind me asking what
happened?

           SARAH
I had a client who decided to sit
down at my table after we finished
and pretended to talk to me, as if he
cared for me. It hit me at a bad time
and I freaked out. There ain't nobody
who pays for sex with a person that
truly cares for that person, so I
broke the freaking chair and kicked
him out.

            JOE
Wait... You ARE a hooker?

           SARAH
I'm actually a Call-Girl... at the
top of the "hooker food chain", if
you will. Usually, I work in New York
City for two weeks, then come back
here for two weeks off, and so on...
But don't worry, you didn't move into
a whore-house. I only did this to
earn some money so I can pay for my
overdue rent.

            JOE
How long have you been a Call-Girl
for?

           SARAH
Been a few years. Since I had a bad
argument with my mother and ran away
from her home in Florida. I've been
on my own ever since, and this is a
way for me to make enough money to
live.

CONTINUED:

                         JOE
              It seems like a dangerous line of
              work, considering today's sexually
              transmitted diseases, and all of the
              shady characters that you must meet
              along the way.

                         SARAH
              Are you talking to me as if you care
              too?

Joe picks up one of the chairs that is laying on the ground
unbroken, and sits on it.

                         JOE
              I sure am. I'm not a client, but I
              would like to be your friend right
              now.

Sarah breaks down in tears.

                         SARAH
              Oh, how I just want to be loved... To
              feel REAL love. I just know that I'll
              never find it. I'll never have my own
              children. I'll never find true
              happiness.

Signaling Sarah to sit down, Joe pulls another chair up to
the table. Sarah sits and puts her head in her hands.

                         JOE
              Do you believe in God?

Sarah peers through her fingers with one eye, while still
holding her head.

                         SARAH
              I do. I just wish he'd show up every
              now and then.

                         JOE
              Do you pray?

Sarah doesn't say anything, as she weeps into her hands.

                         JOE (cont'd)
              Maybe it is time for you to welcome
              him into your life. Beginning with a
              prayer. Not to be judgmental, but
              I'm pretty sure that God would frown
              upon your line of work right now.
                         (MORE)

CONTINUED:

                    JOE (cont'd)
          You've expressed to me how unhappy
          you are doing that, and how it
          hinders what you truly seek, which is
          true love. You can find other work.
          Even if it doesn't pay as well, I
          promise that you'll be more happy.
          When was the last time that you spoke
          with your mother?

Sarah begins to cry uncontrollably. Joe gets up and gives
her a hug.

                    JOE (cont'd)
          Alright, enough of the serious talk.
          Come on, I'll help you clean this
          mess up before the landlord arrives.
          He said that he'll be here today to
          look at my ceiling that caved in on
          me last night.

                    SARAH
          Seriously? He won't do a thing to fix
          it. Everyone who lived in that
          apartment has had issues with the
          ceiling leaking, yet he never does
          crap to deal with it.

                    JOE
          That's what I figured, which is why I
          picked up some ceiling plaster. I'll
          fix it the best I can, then have him
          deduct some money off of my rent.

                    SARAH
          Yeah? Good luck with that.

                                   DISSOLVE TO:

MOMENTS LATER

With his bed and mattress leaning against the wall, Joe is
standing on a chair, patching the ceiling with plaster.
Soon, a leg of the chair gives out and Joe falls to the
ground. He is unhurt, gets up and throws the chair into the
apartment building dumpster outside. It lands atop the
broken chair from Sarah's apartment.

                                   DISSOLVE TO:

LATER THAT NIGHT

Laying in his bed, Joe is awakened by an argument outside
his apartment in the hallway. He hears banging and a window
smashing, and buries his head under his covers.

                                        DISSOLVE TO:

NEXT MORNING

It is cold inside Joe's apartment as he gets out of bed. He
remembers the scuffle outside his apartment door in the
middle of the night, and walks out into the hallway to see
broken glass strewn all over the floor from the window at
the end of the hall, along with a piece of chair backing.
Joe walks to the window and looks down at the dumpster
outside and sees yet another broken chair on top of his and
Sarah's.

<PLAY SONG 'BREAK THE CHAIR'>

                                        FADE TO:

INT. LIVING ROOM MUSIC NIGHTCLUB - EVENING - ONE WEEK LATER

Randy and Joe are behind the bar as Randy is showing Joe the
proper way to slice lemons and limes for drink garnishing.
Joe is wearing a Living Room T-Shirt proudly.

                    JOE
          Randy, I can't thank you enough for
          giving me this job. I do realize that
          I am the first non-family member to
          tend bar at the Living Room.

                    RANDY
          What are you talking about? You ARE
          family! And don't thank me yet. You
          will be working your tail off here,
          beginning tonight. By the time the
          band Missing Persons hits the stage,
          this place will be packed with
          thirsty patrons. It'll be non-stop
          action for several hours, but the
          night will fly by.

                                        (CONTINUED)

CONTINUED:

                    JOE
         I'm ready for the challenge.

                              DISSOLVE TO:

HOURS LATER

The Living Room is packed with music lovers. Joe is
frantically trying to keep up with pouring beers and mixing
drinks, while patrons are heard shouting out their drink
requests over the loud room noise. Handing someone their
change, Joe notices his sister Jade standing beside them,
crying.

                    JOE
         Jade! What is wrong?

                    JADE
         Bill has left home. He is involved
         with someone else and he wants a
         divorce.

                    JOE
         What?! You're kidding right?

                    JADE
         I can't believe it, Joey. I had no
         idea.

The crowd gets louder and more impatient for their drinks as
Joe talks with Jade.

                    JOE
         Jade, it's my first night tending bar
         so I need to keep working, but stick
         around and we can talk in-between
         busy spurts. I am SO sorry to learn
         this. I am in shock.

As Joe moves down the bar to serve more drinks, Jade leaves
the venue.

                              DISSOLVE TO:

INT. PROVIDENCE APARTMENT - NEXT AFTERNOON

Slipping on a Living Room T-Shirt for work later in the day,
Joe walks over to his ringing phone and answers it.

                                        (CONTINUED)

CONTINUED:

                    JOE
          What? No... NO! Tell me you are
          lying... Not Jade... TELL ME!!

Joe begins crying.

                    JOE (cont'd)
          Sleeping pills? Oh... Jade... NO...
          Not JADE!!!

                                        FADE TO:

INT. CHURCH - LATE MORNING, DAYS LATER

A large congregation has gathered for Jade's funeral mass.
Jade's casket sits in front of the altar while the Minister
wraps-up the eulogy.

MINISTER, Grey thinning hair, wearing reading spectacles and
traditional Christian Minister garb.

                    MINISTER
          Before we take our sister Jade to her
          final resting place, her brother Joe
          will say some words in remembrance.

Carrying an acoustic guitar, Joe walks up and lays it on the
ground next to Jade's casket before continuing to the
podium. He adjusts the microphone and begins speaking in a
somber voice.

                    JOE
          I'd like you all to know about my
          sister Jade. She was an outspoken
          person who communicated to everyone
          with an honest freedom. One never
          needed to guess where Jade stood on
          any given subject matter, as she was
          brutally honest with everyone,
          especially herself. I admired her
          curiosity about others, and her
          compassion for them. She was full of
          great humor & wit, and if I ever
          needed to find Jade in a room full of
          people I'd simply follow the
          laughter. When I wasn't following her
          laughter, I'd be getting guided to
          some new group of people by her,
          where she would always begin by
          saying "You all need to meet my
          brother Joey".
                    (MORE)

                                        (CONTINUED)

CONTINUED:

                              JOE (cont'd)
          I used to hate it when she called me
          "Joey", but I never questioned how
          proud she was of me... and I was
          proud to be her little brother. Jade
          encouraged me - stood up for me -
          challenged me, and then cheered me
          on. It was her record collection that
          I'd raid while she endured hours-on-
          end while I pounded my drums to her
          Alice Cooper, Emerson Lake & Palmer,
          Queen and Beatles vinyl. Only once do
          I recall her locking me out of the
          house for a full day so she could get
          some peace & quiet, which was OK
          because I owed her a few days. You
          see, when I was three years old, I
          was sharing a bedroom with my
          youngest sister. I had a total of
          four sisters... FOUR... being the
          only male in the house, I can tell
          you that I never saw the bathroom...
          and on my youngest sister's dresser
          was a bottle of baby aspirin. I LOVED
          the taste of baby aspirins when I was
          three years old, and I proceeded to
          eat the entire large bottle of them
          one Saturday morning before the
          cartoons came on one of the three TV
          stations that were available in those
          days. As I was watching the TV, 10-
          year-old Jade walked into the room
          with the empty aspirin bottle,
          inquiring if I had eaten them. I lied
          and said "no". She explained how it
          was important for me to tell the
          truth because if I ate them and
          didn't tell anyone I could die. I
          began to shake and admitted to the
          overdose. She alerted my father, who
          took me to the hospital for my
          stomach to get pumped. I remember
          that day like it was yesterday...
          when my 10-year-old sister Jade saved
          the life of her 4-year-old "brother
          Joey". How I wish that I was able to
          return the favor to save hers. She
          was my biggest fan. I hope today,
          that she somehow knows that I was HER
          biggest fan... Jade, your laughter
          will echo on in my heart while I
          watch for signs from you until we
          meet again... I love you & miss
          you... your brother Joey.

                                        (CONTINUED)

CONTINUED:

As tears flow throughout the congregation, Joe walks to
Jade's casket, picks up his guitar, and performs a song that
he wrote for her after learning of her death.

<PLAY SONG 'THE WORD BELIEVE'>

                    JOE
                 (singing)
        The sky was grey
        The wind howled as you went away
        Did it dare say even yesterday
        Wasn't made for you and me
        Forget sensible
        While I lay here indefensible
        And the world goes one dimensional
        And I float right off the sea
        You and I believed in a childhood
        That it would always be
        But the word "Believe"
        Is spelled with "L-I-E"
        You were first in class
        When it came to making people laugh
        It's what they wrote upon your
        epitaph
        It's what I think about when I grieve
        You and I believed in living
        That we would always be
        But the word "Believe"
        Is spelled with "L-I-E"
        Now that you're free
        I remember what you said to me
        If you get the chance to fly
        Don't wait up for me
        Then hid your pain under your sleeve
        You and I believed in a Heaven
        This I still believe
        And that God was there
        And it's you that He just received
        The sky was grey
        The wind howled as you went away

Upon completion of the song, Joe leans over and kisses
Jade's casket.

                                        FADE TO:

INT. THE LIVING ROOM MUSIC VENUE - DAYS LATER, EARLY EVENING

Joe is preparing for another busy night of work, as he cuts lemons and limes behind the bar. Randy comes over and shakes his hand.

                    JOE
          Hi Randy. Thanks so much for
          attending Jade's service.

                    RANDY
          I loved Jade. She was an incredible
          woman. And you, my friend, were an
          amazing brother to her.

Randy hands an envelope to Joe.

                    JOE
          What's this, Randy?

                    RANDY
          This may be the ticket to your
          future. I know how you want to record
          your own CD. Well, I think you may
          have written your best songs and that
          it is time to let the world hear
          them. You are booked to record at Sun
          Studio in Memphis next week, where
          Elvis Presley, Johnny Cash and Jerry
          Lee Lewis all recorded. I've heard
          you talk about that studio for as
          long as I've known you. It is your
          time now.

                    JOE
          Are you serious? Oh my God, Randy!

                    RANDY
          There should be enough money in the
          envelope for gas to drive there and
          back, along with some hotel cash.
          Just don't forget about me when you
          make it big.

                    JOE
          I really can't believe that you are
          doing all of this for me. How will I
          even begin to repay you?

                    RANDY
          Just promise that you will only use
          your music for good things.
                    (MORE)

                                        (CONTINUED)

CONTINUED:

                    RANDY (cont'd)
Find a way to better the world
through your melodies and lyrics...
and promise that you'll never forget
the words of your friend, Randy.

                    JOE
Are you kidding me, Randy? I will
always cherish every conversation
that we've had over the years. I
promise you that I will do my best to
change the world for the better.

                    RANDY
That's exactly what I wanted to hear.
You are one of the last great
dreamers. Only true dreamers have the
power to change the world for the
better... And always remember that
THESE are "The good old days", no
matter which day you are living in.

                              FADE TO:

INT. LANSKY'S CLOTHING STORE IN MEMPHIS - LATE MORNING

Searching for the perfect thing to wear for his first night
of recording at Sun Studio, Joe rifles through rack after
rack of colorful and uniquely styled shirts. An elder man
walks over to him.

BERNARD LANSKY, Frail man in his early eighties, thin grey
hair

                    BERNARD LANSKY
Hello there, young man. May I assist
you?

                    JOE
Wow... You are Bernard Lansky, right?

                    BERNARD LANSKY
The one and only... and who are you?

                    JOE
My name is Joe. I saw you in a
documentary that I recently watched.
Is it true that you dressed Elvis
Presley during his musical career?

                    BERNARD LANSKY
I sure did. They call me "The
Clothier to The King".
                    (MORE)

                              (CONTINUED)

CONTINUED:

                    BERNARD LANSKY (cont'd)
Elvis was poorer than dirt when he
first walked into my store. I sent
him away with some clothes and told
him to pay me when he became famous,
and boy, did he ever become famous
and pay me back more than I could
have ever imagined. Elvis was the
most generous person I ever met.

                    JOE
That is so cool... When did you
realize that he was going to be a big
star?

                    BERNARD LANSKY
I could see it when I looked into his
eyes for the first time. That boy had
charisma oozing from his pores. It
was confirmed when he was booked to
perform on the Ed Sullivan Show. I
sent him to New York City with some
of the best threads in my store to
wear, and Elvis was on his way.

                    JOE
That is great. Would you mind helping
me pick out a shirt?

                    BERNARD LANSKY
Of course I'll help. That is my
specialty. What will you be wearing
it for?

                    JOE
Well, I'm a singer and song-writing
musician, too, so I'd like a shirt
that I can wear onstage or in the
recording studio.

                    BERNARD LANSKY
Right this way, Joe.

Bernard heads to a rack of modern shirts and pulls one out
that has a mix of brightly colored stripes on it... yellows,
oranges, and reds.

                    BERNARD LANSKY (cont'd)
Here's your shirt.

                    JOE
That was quick! This is very funky.
Perfect!
                    (MORE)

CONTINUED:

                        JOE (cont'd)
          I'll take it, but I'd love to hear an
          Elvis story before paying for it.

                        BERNARD LANSKY
          Sure. You know, I would deliver
          clothes to Elvis at Graceland all the
          time. I'd go there just after five
          p.m., once I left the clothing shop
          for the day. Several times, Elvis
          would be sitting at his dinner table
          with his family and close friends
          when I arrived. He would always say
          "Bernard, sit down and join us for
          breakfast." I'd always reply by
          saying "Breakfast?! It is after 5
          o'clock! I'm going home to have
          dinner with my wife."... Oh, how I
          wish now that I sat at that table and
          joined Elvis for breakfast one of
          those times. I miss that man more
          than anyone will ever know.

                        JOE
          I can imagine. Would you mind sharing
          with me the address of the apartment
          that Elvis and his parents lived in
          when they were poor? I'd like to
          visit there to see his humble
          beginnings.

                        BERNARD LANSKY
          You're better off going to Graceland
          and taking the tour there. It is a
          lot more interesting.

                        JOE
          I do plan on touring Graceland, but
          I'd rather go there AFTER I record at
          Sun Studio, just like Elvis did.
          Currently, I am starting out poor
          like he did and I'd really like to
          see that portion of his history. I
          can relate to it.

                        BERNARD LANSKY
          Sure, I'll give you the address, but
          wait until you record at Sun Studio
          before you see Graceland? When the
          heck would THAT ever happen?

CONTINUED:

                    JOE
         Actually, tonight... I am recording a
         CD there this week, and my sessions
         begin tonight. I'll be walking into
         Sun wearing this shirt that you just
         picked out for me.

                    BERNARD LANSKY
         Well, in that case, follow me.

Joe follows Mr. Lansky as he goes behind his desk and pulls
out a glossy 8"x10" photo of him and Elvis Presley. He picks
up a black marker and writes on the photo:
"To Joe - Recording at Sun Studio - Why not? - Who else is
doing this? - Your friend, Bernard Lansky"... Mr. Lansky
waves the photo a few times to allow the ink to dry, then
hands it to Joe.

Looking at the photo, Joe begins to shake his head in
disbelief.

                    BERNARD LANSKY (cont'd)
         Is something wrong?

                    JOE
         No, not at all. This is so very cool.
         I am just amazed because my best
         friend always says "Who else is doing
         this" whenever I, or we, are doing
         something very special. I'm just
         blown away that you wrote that.

                    BERNARD LANSKY
         Well, I think it is cool that you are
         recording at Sun. Go make a hit
         record, and pay me for the shirt
         after you have a song on the radio. I
         need a new King to dress, and I can
         see it in your eyes.

                    JOE
         That is tremendously generous of you,
         Mr. Lansky. Thank you very much...
         Oh, I didn't mean to sound like Elvis
         there... Thank you... Thank you very
         much... Actually, I feel a bit uneasy
         about you saying that you need a new
         King to dress. I had read that Elvis
         could be a bit jealous of other
         singers.

                                              (CONTINUED)

CONTINUED:

                    BERNARD LANSKY
          That, he could be... But I'm sure
          that his ghost has mellowed out. Here
          is the address for Elvis' early
          apartment building. Just go to the
          office. They give tours of it daily.
          Now get out of here and record your
          masterpiece.

Mr. Lansky hands Joe a piece of paper.

                    JOE
          I can't thank you enough, Mr. Lansky.
          I'll do what I can to make you, and
          Elvis, proud.

                              DISSOLVE TO:

INT. MANAGER'S OFFICE AT LAUDERDALE COURTS APARTMENTS -
EARLY AFTERNOON

Joe walks into the manager's office and rings the bell that
sits on the counter. He can hear some muffled talking from a
room behind the counter, but nobody responds to the sound of
the bell.

                    JOE
          Hello... Hello?

A woman walks out from the room behind the counter, looking
frustrated that somebody is bothering her.

APARTMENT BUILDING MANAGER, Overweight middle-age woman
eating a donut

                    APARTMENT BUILDING MANAGER
          How may I help you?

                    JOE
          I'd like to tour the apartment that
          Elvis Presley once lived in, please.

                    APARTMENT BUILDING MANAGER
          There ain't no tours today.

The woman turns around and heads back into the room.

                    JOE
               (begging)
          Wait... Please... I walked all the
          way across town to see it. I was told
          that tours are given every day.

                                        (CONTINUED)

CONTINUED:

                    APARTMENT BUILDING MANAGER
               (off screen - voice
                coming from other
                room)
          Well not today. That apartment is
          being cleaned.

                    JOE
          I'll help to clean it!

The woman comes back out from the room.

                    APARTMENT BUILDING MANAGER
          Do I need to call the police to get
          you to leave?

Shaking his head, Joe walks out of the building.

                              DISSOLVE TO:

EXT. SUN STUDIO - LATE AFTERNOON

Carrying his acoustic guitar, Joe stands on the sidewalk
outside the famed Sun recording studio and absorbs the
historic marker that is erected on a post, which reads:

ELVIS PRESLEY AND SUN RECORDS
In July 1954 Sun Records released Elvis Presley's first
recording. That record, and Elvis' four that followed on the
Sun label, changed popular music. Elvis developed an
innovative and different sound combining blues, gospel, and
country. That quality made Elvis a worldwide celebrity
within two years. He went on to become one of the most
famous and beloved entertainers in history. Sun Records
introduced many well known people in all fields of music.
Generations of musicians have been affected by those who
recorded here and especially by the music Elvis Presley
first sang at Sun Records.

                    JOE
          OK world... It's my turn!

                              DISSOLVE TO:

INT. SUN STUDIO CONTROL ROOM - MOMENTS LATER

JAMES LOTT, Main Sun Studio Sound Engineer

                    JAMES LOTT
          Welcome to Sun, Joe.

                                        (CONTINUED)

CONTINUED:

                    JOE
          Thanks so much, James. It is such an
          honor for me to be here.

                    JAMES LOTT
          So, what type of record will we be
          making this week?

                    JOE
          Mostly an acoustic record. Just my
          voice, guitar and piano, and I'll
          sprinkle in some drums here and
          there. I've got seventeen songs that
          I'd like to get recorded here at Sun.

                    JAMES LOTT
          Wow... That is aggressive. Are they
          all original songs?

                    JOE
          Yes, I wrote them all. I'd like to
          achieve a sound similar to Johnny
          Cash's latest CD. Very stark and raw.

                    JAMES LOTT
          Well, that shouldn't be a problem at
          all. Johnny's latest record was
          engineered by a friend of mine, David
          Ferguson. I know his style well. I
          suggest that we begin with the piano
          parts. Let me get the keyboard set up
          here in the control room and we can
          begin tracking.

                    JOE
          Awesome... Would you mind if I look
          around the studio while you do that?

                    JAMES LOTT
          This studio is your studio for the
          next several days. Make yourself at
          home here...

Seeming to study every square foot of the main studio room,
along with all of the photos on the walls and instruments
assembled throughout the space, Joe looks as though he has
just entered Heaven. Eventually, James enters the room.

                    JAMES LOTT (cont'd)
          Quite a magical place, isn't it?

CONTINUED:

>   JOE
>   It seems so surreal to be standing in
>   here, never mind recording my own CD
>   within these walls. Is this THE
>   actual microphone that Elvis sang
>   into?

>   JAMES LOTT
>   Sure is! See that "X" on the floor?
>   That is where Elvis stood when he
>   recorded the vocals on his first hit
>   song 'That's Alright Mama'.

>   JOE
>   Then, that's where I'll stand when we
>   get to the vocal tracks. So cool!

>   JAMES LOTT
>   I've got the keyboard all set up for
>   you to play in the control room. Why
>   don't we head in there and begin to
>   track your seventeen songs.

>   JOE
>   You'll need to pinch me first. This
>   is a dream come true.

The two walk into the control room and Joe sits at the
keyboard, which is set-up just below a large photo of Johnny
Cash. James sits at the sound-board mixing console and
begins to work some buttons and dials.

>   JAMES LOTT
>   OK... We are ready to roll. When you
>   see the tape rolling you may begin to
>   play.

Joe is looking nervous as the tape starts to roll, and he
hits a bad chord as he begins to play.

>   JOE
>   Shoot! Sorry, man. Let's start again.

>   JAMES LOTT
>   Hang on a second. I know exactly what
>   you need.

James walks over to a small refrigerator and pulls out two
beers, handing one to Joe.

>   JAMES LOTT (cont'd)
>   Here, let's chill for a minute before
>   we begin for real.

                                        (CONTINUED)

CONTINUED:

Accepting the beer, Joe chugs down a few large gulps to calm his nerves.

> JAMES LOTT (cont'd)
> You know, my very first session of
> sound engineering here was for the
> band U2. I had the producer from
> their record label on one side of me
> telling me how I should be mixing the
> songs, and Sam Phillips who started
> Sun Studio on the other side of me
> telling me to mix it the exact
> opposite way. It was the most
> stressful session ever, and ever
> since then I try to make sure that
> the artists never feel that way when
> they are within these sacred walls to
> record. They should only feel their
> craft of music within their soul, and
> deliver it right from there onto the
> tape so it reaches the listeners of
> their music at the soul level. Adding
> stress is an unnecessary filter that
> blocks those spiritual energies. When
> you start to feel like your soul is
> ready to record, I'll roll tape
> again.

Finishing his beer, Joe places the empty bottle on the floor near the keyboard stand, tilts his head from side-to-side, and looks at James.

> JOE
> Let's do this.

Over the next 30 minutes, Joe begins to play the keyboard while James works the recording equipment. The process appears to be going smoothly, as Joe indicates to James the tempo speed to set the metronome to prior to the recording of each song. Prior to the fourth song, James injects some motivational words to Joe.

> JAMES LOTT
> You are doing great. I can't wait to
> hear the lyrics and melody that
> you'll add to these piano parts.

> JOE
> Thanks, James... That means a lot to
> me.

(CONTINUED)

CONTINUED:

                    JAMES LOTT
          Seriously, when Elvis Presley first
          recorded here, the songs he sang
          weren't all his original songs, and
          he wasn't playing every instrument on
          the records. What you are doing makes
          you a bit more special.

Joe becomes visibly uneasy with those words.

                    JOE
          I'm not so sure about that, but let's
          keep going while we're on a roll.
          This next song should have a tempo of
          97 beats per minute.

James sets the metronome, turns some dials on the mixing
board, then points at Joe, triggering him to play the next
piano arrangement. For some reason, the sustain pedal on the
keyboard stops working.

                    JOE (cont'd)
          Stop the tape, James. Something isn't
          right with the pedal. There is no
          sustain on the notes anymore.

                    JAMES LOTT
          That's strange. We've never had an
          issue with that pedal before.

James gets out of his chair and begins fidgeting with the
wires that lead in and out of the keyboard and sustain pedal
in effort to bring it back to life. Eventually, he goes over
to a box with several old studio parts in it and pulls out
another sustain pedal and exchanges it with the dead one. He
tickles the keyboard keys while holding down the pedal with
his feet.

                    JAMES LOTT (cont'd)
          Voila! OK... Where were we?

They begin the recording process again, until the
replacement pedal begins doing the same thing, resulting in
no sustain coming out of the keyboard.

                    JOE
          It's doing it again, James.

                    JAMES LOTT
          What the? Maybe it is the keyboard
          itself. Let me call a friend who
          lives nearby to see if we can use his
          electric piano.

CONTINUED:

Joe goes back out into the main studio room to soak up the history of the space until the alternative keyboard arrives. Eventually James calls Joe back into the control room to commence recording.

>   JAMES LOTT (cont'd)
>   So, I matched the piano sound on this
>   keyboard as closely as I could to the
>   one that you were previously
>   recording with. Let's give it another
>   shot.

About halfway through the song, the tape machine stops working.

>   JAMES LOTT (cont'd)
>   What the heck is going on here?

In an attempt to save the recording session, James turns all of the equipment off, waits a few moments, then turns it all back on again. He re-tries the system and everything appears to be working well.

>   JAMES LOTT (cont'd)
>   Well, if at first you don't
>   succeed... or during the second time,
>   try, try again.

Once again, James rolls tape, then points at Joe who begins to play the electric piano. Joe almost gets to the end of the song when that third sustain pedal also quits working. Joe stops and shakes his head. James turns from the mixing board console and looks at Joe, who simply points to the pedal.

>   JAMES LOTT (cont'd)
>   That's IT!! I am done here for
>   tonight. I'm shutting down all of
>   this equipment and letting Elvis'
>   ghost clear out of here. We can begin
>   fresh tomorrow.

>   JOE
>   That sucks. We are loosing a full
>   session of tracking and I am now
>   nervous that we won't get all
>   seventeen songs recorded this week.

>   JAMES LOTT
>   Don't worry. We will make it happen.
>   Let's begin tomorrow at eleven in the
>   morning instead of at six p.m....
>   (MORE)

(CONTINUED)

CONTINUED:

                    JAMES LOTT (cont'd)
We can work straight through the day
and night.

                    JOE
Well, that sounds good to me, but I
don't trust that this equipment will
work any better tomorrow. Is there a
music store where I can purchase an
electric piano sustain pedal in the
morning before coming in here?

                    JAMES LOTT
I don't want you spending your money
on equipment that the studio should
have.

                    JOE
I don't want to leave Memphis without
having my seventeen songs recorded.
The pedal will be a donation from me
to Sun.

                              DISSOLVE TO:

INT. MEMPHIS MUSIC STORE - NEXT MORNING (EARLY)

A potential young customer is banging on a drum set in the
middle of the store as a music store clerk places two
keyboard sustain pedals on the counter in front of Joe, who
is trying to listen to the young player and the store clerk
at the same time.

                    MUSIC STORE CLERK
These are the two pedals that I have.
What kind of keyboard are you
playing?

                    JOE
I'm not sure. The keyboard belongs to
the recording studio that I'm
recording in. I don't have a lot of
money so I'll just take the less
expensive one, please.

                    MUSIC STORE CLERK
I wish it were that easy. They are
forty dollars each. The problem is
that each of these pedals are
configured differently, with each
matching up to one or the other kind
of keyboard.
                    (MORE)

                              (CONTINUED)

CONTINUED:

                    MUSIC STORE CLERK (cont'd)
          If you plug the wrong one in, it will
          have sustain the entire time except
          for when you hold it down, which is
          the opposite of the norm.

                         JOE
          Yeah, that would really mess with my
          ability to play my parts well.

Distracted by the fact that the young kid playing the drums
keeps hitting the rims of each drum as he plays, Joe pauses
for a moment.

                    MUSIC STORE CLERK
          So, what would you like to do?

                         JOE
                    (counting his money)
          Would it be possible for me to pay
          for one pedal, but take both to see
          which one works, then bring the other
          one back after my session?

                    MUSIC STORE CLERK
          I'm sorry, but that is against our
          policy.

                         JOE
          But, I'm recording over at Sun
          Studio. You could even come in and
          check the place out while I'm
          recording.

                    MUSIC STORE CLERK
          Dude, I've taken every friend that
          visits from out of town on the tour
          of Sun. I've been in Sun so much that
          I'm beginning to get a sunburn. I
          can't do it.

Joe notices that the mother of the young drummer is telling
the salesman that is with them they will need to go back to
another music store where her son had an easier time playing
a drum set there. They begin to walk away from the drums and
toward the door.

                         JOE
          You are losing a big drum set sale
          right now. What if I make the sale
          for you? Would you allow me to take
          both pedals for the price of one?

                                            (CONTINUED)

CONTINUED:

                    MUSIC STORE CLERK
          If you can make that sale right now I
          will GIVE both of these pedals to
          you.

                    JOE
          Deal.

Joe walks over to the woman and her son.

                    JOE (cont'd)
          You are a pretty good drummer. I'm a
          drummer myself, and when I was about
          your age I would hit the rims a lot
          because I hadn't adjusted my drums
          correctly. It sounded like you were
          experiencing the same issue. If you
          don't mind, sit down at the drum set
          again and I'll adjust them for your
          size, OK?

The boy sits behind the drums again and Joe has him hold a
pair of drum sticks and hit each drum several times with
each hand as Joe makes angle and height adjustments to the
set.

                    JOE (cont'd)
          OK, now play the same beats that you
          were playing before.

The young boy's face lights up as his arms make his way
around the drum set in a flurry of various beats. He
eventually stops and turns to his mother.

                    YOUNG DRUMMER
          This is the one for sure, Mom! Can we
          get it?

Joe walks back toward the counter and stands with the music
store clerk who has his hands on each sustain pedal. They
watch together as the floor salesperson discusses the price
with the young drummer's mother. They shake hands and the
salesperson begins filling out a sales-slip on a clipboard.
The music store clerk picks up the pedals and hands them to
Joe.

                    MUSIC STORE CLERK
          Have a great session at Sun, man.

                              DISSOLVE TO:

INT. SUN STUDIO MAIN RECORDING ROOM - LATE MORNING

Standing on the "X" where Elvis Presley stood while
recording his songs, Joe quietly says a prayer while holding
onto Elvis' microphone.

                    JOE
          Dear God, please allow my recording
          sessions to run smoothly from this
          point forward. I promise to promote
          only good things through the music
          that I write and record... and if
          Elvis is with you, please let him
          know that I will do everything I can
          to keep his memory alive whenever I
          speak about my sessions at Sun
          Studio.

James walks into the main room from the control room.

                    JAMES LOTT
          Great news! One of the sustain pedals
          works perfectly on the studio's
          keyboard, and the other one is what
          is needed for my friend's electric
          piano, so that all worked out well.

                    JOE
          Awesome!

                    JAMES LOTT
          Alright, let's get back to work. This
          will be a long day and night.

The scene goes back and forth from Joe recording piano parts
in the control room to recording acoustic guitar and
drumming parts in the main studio room, as well as cuts to
James and Joe eating a pizza at one point, having a beer at
another point, and various cut-aways to a clock's hands
spinning around until the end of the scene shows the clock's
hands at 2:30am.

                    JAMES LOTT (cont'd)
          I think we'd better both get out of
          here and get some sleep. You kicked
          butt with laying all of the
          instrument parts down today.

                    JOE
          And YOU kicked butt engineering it
          for all of these hours. I can't thank
          you enough for the time and attention
          that you are putting into my project.

                                        (CONTINUED)

CONTINUED:

>   JAMES LOTT
>   That's what I'm here for. I've got
>   your back, and your record is going
>   to be great.

>   JOE
>   I'm really looking forward to adding
>   the vocals tomorrow. That's what
>   makes these songs come to life.

>   JAMES LOTT
>   You mean to say "today"... You'll be
>   adding vocals today. It's almost
>   three o'clock in the morning. Get out
>   of here and get those vocal cords to
>   bed. Let's meet back here at noon.

>   FADE TO:

INT. MEMPHIS HOTEL ROOM - NEXT MORNING

A beam of sunlight hits Joe's face, wakening him from a
short night of sleep. He looks at the digital clock near the
bed, which reads 10:34am, and gets out of bed. As he gathers
clothes to wear from his suitcase he notices a card stuffed
in the pair of jeans that he chooses.

>   JOE
>   (talking to himself)
>   This is the card from Jade when I
>   left for Los Angeles. I don't
>   remember ever placing it into my
>   suitcase. Hmm.

Joe opens the card and reads it once again...

"Dear Joe,
I hope that you always follow the SUN, and that it leads you
on a journey through your dream. I'll be with you in spirit
with every song that you sing!
Love,
Jade"

>   JOE (cont'd)
>   Wow... You ARE with me, Jade... and
>   today we sing IN the SUN!

He places the card on the bed, grabs the clothes that he
picked out, and heads toward the shower while practicing
some vocal exercises.

>   CUT TO:

INT. SUN STUDIO MAIN RECORDING ROOM - NOON

James is adjusting the microphone in front of Joe's mouth, while Joe positions himself on the "X" on the floor that marks the spot where Elvis Presley had recorded his vocals.

                    JAMES LOTT
          So, what is this first song about?

                    JOE
          It stems from one of my earliest
          memories. I was about three years
          old, and on my street lived a very
          old man. The oldest person that my
          sisters and I had ever known. His
          house was also very old and falling
          apart, and he had a pear tree in his
          front yard. Every day, he would sit
          on his decrepit porch while all of us
          neighborhood kids would talk about
          how he must be a warlock or
          something. We'd dare each other to
          run up and steal a pear from his
          tree, which we all believed to be
          poisonous. His name was Old Andrew,
          and as I got older and looked back on
          my childhood, I regret not ever
          speaking with him, as he must have
          been a very lonely man. For this
          song, I changed the gender of the
          character, and titled it 'Mrs.
          Barker'...

                    JAMES LOTT
          What an interesting song subject.
          Well, let's get the lyrics on tape,
          shall we?

                    JOE
          Absolutely! This is a moment that
          I've waited a long time for!

James heads into the control room while Joe slips on a pair of headphones.

                    JAMES LOTT
                 (speaking through
                 Joe's headphones)
          OK! Let's take it from the top.

The music begins to play in Joe's headphones, but Joe stops the process before singing any vocals.

                                        (CONTINUED)

CONTINUED:

                         JOE
          James, I'm sorry... Give me just one
          minute.

Taking off his headphones, Joe heads over to the piano in
the corner of the room. He takes out the card from Jade,
standing it on top of the piano so as if to give it a full
view of the session. He walks back to the "X" on the floor
and places the headphones back over his ears.

                    JOE (cont'd)
          Thanks James. I'm ready now.

The music re-starts in his headphones, Joe takes a sip of
water and sings the lyrics into the microphone.

<PLAY SONG 'MRS.BARKER'>

CONTINUED:

"At seven o'clock in the morning
There's a raven at Mrs. Barker's door
The kids tell tales of Mrs. Barker's skeletons
Inside on the sofa
Sits a lonely ghost who wants to talk
But outside in her yard the trees are poisonous
The window opens - The kids say Shhhh...
A raven takes a bite
Of an apple black as coal
That Mrs. Barker holds
We all know Mrs. Barker
But who's gonna ring her doorbell
If she sees you run away
She's gonna cast her spell
Poor old Mrs. Barker are you well
Poor old Mrs. Barker are you well
The sun is getting higher
The raven sits on a telephone wire
Daring all the kids below to throw stones
The porch cat's gonna hiss
If in walks the man with the grocery list
So he keeps the change
And leaves some bags on the front steps
The door opens - The kids say Shhhh...
She looks up in the sky
Even the sun snuck away
As she drags the bags inside
We all know Mrs. Barker
But who's gonna ring her doorbell
We'd all like to help her
But would we live to tell
Poor old Mrs. Barker are you well
Poor old Mrs. Barker are you well
At seven o'clock this morning
No raven came to Barker's door
The kids tell tales of Mrs. Barker laying there
The grocery man has no bags in his hands
The kids stare in a daze
As the raven in the sky
Just circles around the place
We all knew Mrs. Barker
But who's gonna ring her doorbell
We'd all like to help her
But would we live to tell
Poor old Mrs. Barker are you well
Poor old Mrs. Barker are you well"

CONTINUED:

                    JAMES LOTT
                (speaking through
                Joe's headphones
                with a choked-up
                voice)
        Come on in to hear the play-back.

Joe walks into the control room to find James wiping his
eyes.

                    JOE
        Dude, what's wrong?

                    JAMES LOTT
        Man, that song just hit me. It
        reminded me of an old lady who lived
        in our neighborhood in Florida when I
        was a kid. Same thing - she was so
        old that we all thought she was some
        sort of a witch. Her house had metal
        louvers over each window and we would
        torment her by throwing small stones
        at them. Each stone would make such a
        loud sound against her metal window
        guards. She must have been so scared
        in there. Your song took me right
        back to my childhood, and I now feel
        bad that we did that. I hadn't
        thought about those days in
        decades... Wow.

Not knowing what to say, Joe just stands there for a few
seconds while James wipes his eyes again.

                    JOE
        I'm really sorry, James.

                    JAMES LOTT
        No. Don't be. I'll bet that many
        people have a "Mrs. Barker" from
        their days of youth. I think that
        lots of folks will connect with that
        song... (clears throat)... Alright.
        That vocal take sounded good to me.
        Anything you want to do over?

                    JOE
        No, I'm OK with that take. One down,
        sixteen to go.

                    JAMES LOTT
        What is the next song you'd like to
        tackle?

                                        (CONTINUED)

CONTINUED:

                    JOE
             Let's do "If Today". It is one of the
             many songs I wrote after getting my
             heart ripped out by my former fiance.
             It's a song about that feeling of
             having no tomorrow after losing love.
             Boy, am I glad I did have many
             tomorrows after her. Today is one of
             my favorite days ever.

Back at the "X" in front of the microphone, Joe sings 'If
Today':

<PLAY SONG 'IF TODAY'>

"If Today you forgot
That I would die for you here on the spot
I'll write down your name and I Love You
Dipping my pen in the blood of my heart
If Today you were gone
Well it's a shame that in vain I was born
Weaving wool for the eyes of a stranger
With the threads of my tapestry torn
Then tomorrow I can't find a dawn
If Today you grew up
Leaving me here as a child
Playing house pretending you're with me
But making believe gets old after a while
Then tomorrow I can't find a smile
Rose tinted glasses wilt in flames of passion I know
But how can you see double where I see one in a row
If Today fell apart
Hours fell off of a clock
Minutes sweep into piles of seconds
If calling you mine is something you're not
Then tomorrow is nothing I've got
If Today"

Joe walks back into the control room where he and James
listen to the play-back of the recording.

                JAMES LOTT
             Now THAT'S a window to someone's
             hurting soul if I ever heard one.
             Wow... Are you OK?

                    JOE
             Yeah, man. I'm OK. Now that I think
             of it, this CD is mostly made up of
             songs that reflect pain.

(CONTINUED)

CONTINUED:

                        JAMES LOTT
          Seriously, Joe, if all of your songs
          are as well written as the first few,
          you really need to get a major
          producer or agent to handle you. Your
          songs need to get out there and
          you'll be on your way to wherever
          you'd like to go.

                        JOE
          Wow, man... That really means a lot
          coming from you. I mean, you've
          worked with so many big stars that
          have recorded here at Sun. Your words
          are kind-of blowing me away right
          now, and I don't want to jinx
          anything, so let's tackle the next
          fifteen songs.

Taking his position in front of the microphone, Joe slips on
the headphones once again. The camera cuts between various
angles of Joe singing in the main studio room and James
mixing on the sound board in the control room, while a clock
with spinning hands is superimposed on the screen, until it
stops at 2:00am.

Sitting together in the control room, James and Joe are each
enjoying a beer and re-capping their recording session.

                        JOE (cont'd)
          James, I can't thank you enough for
          all the work that you did on my
          recordings, and the level of detail
          that you put into it.

                        JAMES LOTT
          It was my absolute pleasure. I didn't
          know much about who you were or what
          your music was about when you first
          stepped foot into Sun, but I now feel
          that I have a friend for life in you.

                        JOE
          Aww, me, too, James.

                        JAMES LOTT
          I also feel that you have the
          potential to go as far as you want to
          in this business. You gave birth to a
          lot of songs here this week. Go out
          there and nurture them. If you do,
          these songs will get big, and so will
          you.

(CONTINUED)

CONTINUED:

James scribbles something onto a piece of paper, and hands
it to Joe, along with a hand-full of CD's.

>   JOE
> What's this?

>   JAMES LOTT
> The CD's are a rough mix of all the
> songs that you recorded here. I was
> mixing them as we went along. On that
> paper is the date, time, and address
> of your show in New York City on your
> way home.

>   JOE
> What?

>   JAMES LOTT
> When we took our dinner break
> earlier, I contacted an old friend of
> mine who books The Bitter End in New
> York City.

>   JOE
> That place is famous. It is where
> Neil Diamond, Bob Dylan, and so many
> other stars got their start.

>   JAMES LOTT
> Well, it is where you will be getting
> your fresh start as a solo artist.
> You've got a few days to drive there.
> You'll be opening for some of the
> musicians from the 'Late Show with
> David Letterman'.

>   JOE
> How exciting! I've been a fan of that
> show and band forever! Wow!! First, I
> must stop at Graceland tomorrow and
> then I'll hit the road. Thanks so
> much for doing that for me.

>   JAMES LOTT
> Just don't forget little old me when
> you hit it big.

>   JOE
> Never!

The two get out of their chairs and give each other a hug.

>   DISSOLVE TO:

EXT. GRACELAND (ELVIS PRESLEY'S ESTATE) - LATE MORNING

A tour guide is addressing a group of fifteen people outside
the front door of Graceland. It is a beautiful sunny day.

                    TOUR GUIDE
          Thank you for visiting us at
          Graceland today, folks. The estate
          was purchased by Elvis Presley in
          March of 1957. He paid $102,500 for
          the house and the 13.8 acres
          surrounding it. Before we walk into
          the house, I do need to let you know
          that we do not allow any food or
          drinks inside, nor is flash
          photography allowed. Please follow me
          into the foyer area.

                              DISSOLVE TO:

INT. TROPHY BUILDING (GRACELAND) - SEVERAL MOMENTS LATER

The tourist group is taking in all of the Elvis Presley
memorabilia that is exhibited around the room, hanging on
walls and presented in display cases.

                    TOUR GUIDE
          This building was originally used by
          Elvis for his slot-car race track,
          which was one of Elvis' many hobbies.
          Eventually it was remodeled to
          display several of Elvis' trophies.
          In this room you will find gold and
          platinum records, the three Grammy
          Awards that Elvis won, personal
          copies of his movie scripts, and even
          the leather suit that Mr. Presley
          wore in his televised '68 Comeback
          Special.

Hovering over a display case, a random tourist raises her
hand and shouts out a question.

                    TOURIST
          Excuse me. What are all of these
          checks for that are on display in
          this case?

                                (CONTINUED)

CONTINUED:

                    TOUR GUIDE
          That is a great question. Every year,
          Elvis would set aside an entire day
          and write out checks to his favorite
          charities. Elvis was a very generous
          man, as you can see by some of the
          checks on display in that case. Among
          his favorite entities to donate to
          was St. Jude's Children's Hospital,
          located right here in Memphis.

Joe walks over to the display case of checks and is visibly
impressed by Elvis' generosity.

                    JOE
               (talking to himself)

          I don't think that I'd be able to
          give away that kind of money in my
          lifetime, even if I WAS rich.

All of a sudden, a strange sound is audible, which seems to
emulate a freight train passing by outside.

                    TOUR GUIDE
          Now, we will go outside to see Elvis'
          grave, which is right next to those
          of his parents.

                    JOE
               (talking to himself)
          Wow. Now I get to go before the King
          of Rock & Roll. I think I've earned
          the privilege by now being a Sun
          Studio Recording Artist, just like
          Elvis was.

The train-like sound grows intensively louder, now
enveloping the entire building, especially through the roof.
The tour guide opens the door and gives a gasp of surprise.

                    TOUR GUIDE
          Whoa!! We won't be going outside yet.
          Wasn't it a beautiful and sunny day
          today? It is now like a monsoon out
          there!

Everyone in the tour group takes turns looking out the door
at the unbelievable down-pouring of rain, which appears to
be falling at a harder and harder pace with each passing
second, with water now cascading over every gutter at
Graceland as they can't handle the volume of water dropping
from the sky.

                                        (CONTINUED)

CONTINUED:

                    JOE
              (talking to himself)
         Man, I hope we can get to Elvis'
         grave soon. I really want to hit the
         road so I won't have to rush to make
         it to New York City in time for my
         show.

Rain gets even more intense...

                    JOE (cont'd)
              (talking quietly in
               prayer)
         God, PLEASE make this rain stop. I
         promise to help one of the charities
         that Elvis donated to, like St.
         Jude's Children's Hospital, with my
         music. Please help me to get my music
         out there so I can make a difference
         in the world. And if Elvis is there
         with you, please let him know that I
         will always give mention of him
         whenever conversing with others about
         my time at Sun Studio and Graceland.

All of a sudden the rain stops. Not a slow-down from a
pouring down to steady rain to drizzle, but a quick stop to
the rain as if someone turned a water faucet off.

                    TOUR GUIDE
         Now THAT is more like it! Please
         follow me folks.

Everyone files out of the trophy room.

                    JOE
         Wow... that was amazing.

                                   DISSOLVE TO:

EXT. GRACELAND PARKING LOT - MOMENTS LATER

On his way to his car, Joe notices a small radio station
building next to the Elvis Presley gift shop. As he is
reading the building's sign, 'Elvis Radio', a man standing
in front of the station begins a conversation with Joe.

RADIO DISC JOCKEY, Middle-age man wearing an Elvis Radio
golf shirt

                    RADIO DISC JOCKEY
         Hey there! Where ya from?

                                        (CONTINUED)

CONTINUED:

                    JOE
          Hi. I'm from Rhode Island.

                    RADIO DISC JOCKEY
          Cool! What brings you to Memphis?

                    JOE
          I've been recording a CD at Sun
          Studio this week.

                    RADIO DISC JOCKEY
          What?! Are you kidding me?

                    JOE
          Not at all. I'm a singer and
          songwriter.

                    RADIO DISC JOCKEY
          Would you mind doing a world-wide
          interview with me on Elvis Radio
          right now?

                    JOE
          Really? That would be great.

The two head into the radio station, where Joe is directed
to a blue chair in front of a microphone. Joe sits down and
the disc jockey takes his place in front of another
microphone.

                    RADIO DISC JOCKEY
          OK, let me write down your name so I
          don't mess it up over the airwaves.

                    JOE
          I'm Joe Silva. S-I-L-V-A

                    RADIO DISC JOCKEY
          Got it. How do you like our blue
          suede chairs, Joe?

                    JOE
          Ha Ha! They are lovely.

                    RADIO DISC JOCKEY
          What is one of your favorite Sun
          Studio recordings of Elvis Presley.

                                              (CONTINUED)

CONTINUED:

                    JOE
          I think that they're all great, but I
          recently heard 'Blue Moon of
          Kentucky' and thought that Elvis did
          a really good rendition of that at
          Sun.

                    RADIO DISC JOCKEY
          Cool. Please place those headphones
          in front of you on your head.

Joe slips the headphones over his ears and adjusts the
broadcast microphone to a comfortable position.

                    RADIO DISC JOCKEY (cont'd)
          Can you hear me OK in your head-set?

                    JOE
          Loud and clear.

                    RADIO DISC JOCKEY
          Great. We go live in about twenty
          seconds when this song ends. At the
          end of the interview I will play
          'Blue Moon of Kentucky'.

                    JOE
          Awesome.

Flipping a few switches as the song fades, the disc jockey
begins the interview by speaking into his microphone.

INTERVIEW BEGINNING

                    RADIO DISC JOCKEY
          This is Elvis fan numero uno, just
          hanging out here inside your radio...
          And here is Joe Silva, Recording
          Artist recording over at Sun Studio
          this week. How's it going over there?

                    JOE
          Oh, it's been great. It's very
          exciting. I'm working with the Sun
          Studio sound engineer that has worked
          with everyone from Jerry Lee Lewis to
          Paul Simon, so it's quite an
          experience over there.

                    RADIO DISC JOCKEY
          Is it all original music?

CONTINUED:

                    JOE
It's all original. There are
seventeen new cuts that I'm doing
this week.

               RADIO DISC JOCKEY
What's it like recording over at Sun
Studio?

                    JOE
It's amazing. It is half focusing on
what needs to get done while the
other half is soaking up the
atmosphere. I mean, there is so much
history there, as you know, so it is
hard to soak it all up in a one-week
session.

               RADIO DISC JOCKEY
I think that most people don't
realize that Sun is still an active
recording studio as well as a tourist
attraction.

                    JOE
It is, and what happens is the studio
is open seven days a week for tours
until six-thirty, so our sessions
actually begin at six-thirty in the
evening, and we spend daytime doing
overdubs and some mixing.

               RADIO DISC JOCKEY
While the tours are going on?

                    JOE
Yes, when the tours are happening,
but we are in the control room where
the folks don't go.

               RADIO DISC JOCKEY
Where Sam Phillips was!

                    JOE
Yes, where Sam was! Here's an
interesting tidbit... If you walk
into Sun Studio and look at the
ceiling, you'll notice that it has
these "V" shapes that hang down with
all of the acoustical tiles that are
stuck to it.
                    (MORE)

CONTINUED:

                    JOE (cont'd)
          When Sam Phillips designed that
          studio room, he had found an old
          speaker box that had "V" shapes
          inside of it, along the back of the
          box, so he decided to design the room
          like a speaker box facing down.

                    RADIO DISC JOCKEY
          Interesting. Very cool. Better than
          egg cartons.

                    JOE
          It really is... it's effective. You
          walk into there an you can actually
          feel the compression on your own
          voice when you speak.

                    RADIO DISC JOCKEY
          Very interesting that you would say
          that, and it's very true. The sound
          of that place has been talked about
          for years... That is was a unique
          sound in Sun Studio.

                    JOE
          And people still come to soak it up.
          Tom Petty's been there, Ringo
          Starr... I mean, the list goes on and
          on.

                    RADIO DISC JOCKEY
          Everybody goes to Sun eventually.
          Well, let's play an Elvis song that
          was recorded at Sun. I think it's one
          of your favorites, right?

                    JOE
          I do... I love it. It's 'Blue Moon of
          Kentucky'.

                    RADIO DISC JOCKEY
          On Elvis Radio with Joe Silva. Thanks
          for dropping by.

                    JOE
          Thanks for having me Jim.

END OF INTERVIEW

'Blue Moon of Kentucky' plays through the radio station's
speakers as Jim and Joe take their headphones off.

(CONTINUED)

CONTINUED:

                    RADIO DISC JOCKEY
Man, you've got a great radio voice.

                    JOE
That was a lot of fun. Thanks for the
opportunity.

                    RADIO DISC JOCKEY
Well, you've got an open invitation
to come back to Elvis Radio anytime.
Let's get you back on the air when
your record comes out.

                    JOE
I'll plan on that.

                                    FADE TO:

INT. THE BITTER END MUSIC VENUE (NYC) - EVENING (2 DAYS
LATER)

Most of the audience seats are taken, with some additional
people standing along one side wall of the historical music
venue, as Joe gets ready to perform his last song onstage.

                    JOE
It has been a thrill for me to
perform here at The Bitter End for
all of you tonight. One of the main
influences on me as a songwriter has
been Neil Diamond, and to stand here
on the same stage where he first
performed publicly is a great honor
for me. I recall hearing Neil say
somewhere that for a person to write
a great song, they need only to look
into their own lives and experiences.
I will leave you with a song that was
derived from an experience I had. It
was late at night, and I was in a
venue similar to this one, but in my
home state of Rhode Island. An
acquaintance of mine came into the
venue and ordered a round of tequila
for the small crowd of folks that
were seated at the bar. I asked him
what the occasion was, and he
informed me that he was heading to
war in the Middle East the next
morning and didn't know when, or even
if, he'd be back. From that point in
the night, I bought the shots.
                  (MORE)

                                  (CONTINUED)

CONTINUED:

> JOE (cont'd)
> The next day, I was watching the news
> and it had some film coverage of his
> ship leaving port out of Rhode
> Island. I recalled him telling me
> that the hardest part about going off
> to war is leaving his mother, kids
> and wife behind. I picked up my
> acoustic guitar and a pen, then wrote
> this song from a soldier's point of
> view. It is called 'Letters From
> War', and I dedicate it to everyone
> here that has served in the military.

The audience claps, and Joe begins his song.

<PLAY SONG 'LETTERS FROM WAR'>

"Well you wrote that you are scared
Baby I'm scared too
I tried to stop a friend from dying
The blood just soaked right through
This war's been so damned long
I stopped counting days
What helps me face another
Are pictures of you I save
But you're miles away bringing up our child alone
Being away from you like this
Is the hardest thing I've ever known
But I'm thinking of when we'll be together again
So baby don't start crying
Your strength is what I need the most
Promise me your eyes are drying
Tell junior that daddy loves you both
Mom when I was young
The war was Vietnam
You taught me how to pray
So they might come back unharmed
But I've grown up now - it's my turn
Say one more for me
While I'm fighting for my family, friends
And my dignity
Mom I never lied I never stole
But if I take a soldier's life
Would God forgive my soul
When all through life you taught me right
So mother don't start crying
I'm trying hard to make you proud
You used to say when times are trying
A bright sun will clear these passing clouds
So be strong now..."

CONTINUED:

Audience applauds.

DISSOLVE TO:

INT. BITTER END DRESSING ROOM - MOMENTS LATER

Joe is in the dressing room of The Bitter End, putting his
guitar in its case and winding up the instrument cable. In
walks the drummer of the 'Late Show with David Letterman'.

RECORD PRODUCER, Drummer for T.V.'s The Late Show

                    RECORD PRODUCER
          Oh... Hello. I'm sorry, I am looking
          to see if my band-mates are here yet.

Recognizing the person as one of his favorite drummers,
Joe's face lights up with excitement.

                    JOE
          Hi. The dressing room is yours. I
          finished my show a little while ago,
          and will be heading to the front of
          the stage to watch your performance.
          I'm a big fan of yours.

                    RECORD PRODUCER
          Oh, thanks. I'm sorry that I missed
          your set. I see that you have an
          acoustic guitar, so I'm guessing that
          you're a singer/songwriter?

                    JOE
          I am, even though my main instrument
          has been drums since I was a child. I
          actually grew up listening to your
          work. You've been a major influence
          on me. Especially the drumming that
          you did on KISS records. They were my
          favorite band when I was young.

                    RECORD PRODUCER
          I'm glad that I had a positive impact
          on you. Yeah, doing the KISS albums
          was a strange feeling, considering
          everyone thought that Peter Chriss
          was doing the drumming. It wasn't
          until years later that it was
          exposed.

CONTINUED:

                    JOE
        I can imagine, especially considering
        'I Was Made For Loving You' became
        their biggest-selling song ever.

                    RECORD PRODUCER
        Those sessions for the KISS 'Dynasty'
        album were a lot of fun.

                    JOE
        Considering all of the artists that
        you've worked in the studio with over
        the years, I imagine that you've been
        in so many great recording studios.
        Which is your favorite for tracking
        drums?

                    RECORD PRODUCER
        Actually, my home studio in The
        Hamptons, in my opinion. I took my
        time with setting it up, and I truly
        believe that my best sounding drum
        tracks come out of that room.
        Speaking of KISS, I actually just
        recorded some drums for Ace Frehley's
        upcoming record in my studio. I'm
        really getting into producing more
        these days, and recently recorded my
        own CD with various singers, such as
        Brian Wilson of the Beach Boys and
        Aaron Neville.

                    JOE
        That is awesome! I just recorded at
        Sun Studio in Memphis over the past
        week, but mostly guitar, piano, and
        my voice. I only peppered the songs
        with a bit of some drums.

                    RECORD PRODUCER
        Sun Studio? Very cool. What kind of
        music do you write?

Joe digs through his backpack and pulls out one of the CD
copies from his Sun sessions, and hands it to the record
producer.

                    JOE
        Here is an un-mastered copy of my
        sessions at Sun. I think that the
        style is Adult Contemporary, but I'll
        let you judge for yourself.
                    (MORE)

(CONTINUED)

CONTINUED:

                    JOE (cont'd)
          I would LOVE for you to add some
          drumming of your own to any of the
          songs, if you deem them worthy.

                    RECORD PRODUCER
          I can't promise you anything, but
          I'll give the songs a listening to.
          Nice chatting with you.

                    JOE
          Thanks so much for taking time to do
          that. My phone number is on the case.
          I'm going to try and find a seat near
          the stage. Have a great show!

Joe exits the dressing room.

                                        FADE TO:

INT. PROVIDENCE APARTMENT - LATE AFTERNOON (NEXT DAY)

The phone inside Joe's apartment is ringing as he enters his
apartment with his guitar and suitcase. He places the items
on the ground and answers the phone.

                    JOE
          Hello.

                    DONNY
               (off screen)
          Joe! You're home, finally. I've been
          trying to reach you for the past day,
          but your answering machine must be
          broke.

Joe looks at the answering machine and sees that it is
blinking "Messages Full".

                    JOE
          That's weird. My answering machine
          says it is full. I know that I've
          been away for a week, but it usually
          holds at least a hundred messages
          before reaching its capacity. I'm
          just getting in.

                                        (CONTINUED)

CONTINUED:

                    DONNY
                (off screen)
        I'd love to hear all about your trip
        and the recording sessions at Sun,
        but I'll bet that your answering
        machine is full because of what I'm
        about to tell you. I've got some
        terrible news to share with you.

                    JOE
        What news?

                    DONNY
                (off screen)
        Turn on your television set.

                    JOE
        To which station?

                    DONNY
                (off screen)
        Any local station.

Walking over to the T.V. with concern, Joe turns it on to
see news coverage of his friend Randy's (of The Living Room)
tragic death. He blankly stares at the television.

                    JOE
        This can't be true.

Joe changes the channel, only to find more coverage on that
station of Randy's demise. Turning the dial again, he finds
another reporter talking about his friend, Randy, and Joe
takes a few steps back and falls onto his bed in shock while
still holding the phone to his ear.

                    NEWS REPORTER
        It is unclear why Randy stopped his
        vehicle on the side of the road, but
        the well-liked owner of The Living
        Room was struck and killed by a
        passing vehicle when he stepped out
        of his car. His wife sent out a
        statement late yesterday, saying that
        she and her family have forgiven the
        driver of the vehicle that struck
        Randy. She said that she recognizes
        how terrible that driver must be
        feeling, and encourages all of
        Randy's friends to forgive him, too.

(CONTINUED)

CONTINUED:

                    JOE
          I can't believe this. I just can't
          believe this. Oh my God. Randy.

Placing his head in one hand, Joe continues to hold the
phone to his other ear while Donny brings him up to speed
regarding news coverage and services for Randy.

                    DONNY
               (off screen)
          I'm sorry, man. I can't believe it
          either. This is all they've been
          talking about on the news. They keep
          showing person after person giving
          testimony of how Randy has helped
          them in one way or another. He truly
          was a remarkable man. The wake will
          be tomorrow at four in the afternoon,
          and his funeral is scheduled for the
          next morning.

                              DISSOLVE TO:

INT./EXT. JOE'S CAR - MID AFTERNOON

Driving down the road, Joe slows his car as he approaches a
policeman re-directing traffic. He rolls down his window as
he stops his car near the officer.

                    JOE
          Hello, Officer, I am just trying to
          get to a wake at the the funeral home
          about a mile up ahead.

                    POLICEMAN
          I think that everyone else in the
          state is attending the same wake,
          which is why I need to have folks
          pull their vehicles down this side-
          street and find parking in this
          neighborhood. There is no more
          parking anywhere close to the funeral
          home.

                    JOE
          Oh... OK. Thank you, sir.

                              DISSOLVE TO:

EXT. FUNERAL HOME - MOMENTS LATER

As he approaches the funeral home by foot, Joe can see that there is a line of people in the front of the building waiting to get in. Getting closer, he notices that the line wraps around the side of the funeral home, and as he keeps walking in search of the end of the line, he follows it as the line wraps around yet the back of the building, then continues along the sidewalk of the street for another quarter-mile or so. As he walks past the several hundred people assembled in the line, he over-hears pieces of conversations praising or quoting Randy...

"Randy coached all of my boys in Little League, and he was THE best influence on them."

"Randy took a lot of foster children into his home when there was nobody else to care for them."

"I didn't know Randy well, but he held a benefit concert at his nightclub when he heard that my daughter was in the hospital and we had no health insurance."

"He would always say that THESE are the good old days, and he was right."

Tears begin to stream down Joe's face from behind his sunglasses as he continues toward the back of the line. He hears Randy's voice echoing in his head, saying "The only thing we leave behind is our reputation."

                    JOE
               (speaking to himself)
          The only thing we leave behind is our
          reputation is right, Randy. Look at
          the one that you've left behind.
          Amazing, my friend.

Joe reaches the end of the line, and the scene is a time-lapse of him inching his way closer to the funeral home entrance over the course of five hours (there is a visual transition from sunshine to evening darkness). This scene dissolves to the next morning as Randy's casket is being carried out of a church and placed into a hearse. Attached to the top of if is his trademark tan baseball hat with the over-sized brim. The scene then cuts to the hearse driving past people along the road holding "We Love You Randy" and "R.I.P. Randy" signs, as well as a theater with the words "May God Bless Randy" displayed on the marquis. The camera pans away to an aerial shot, which shows a funeral procession of cars that is several miles long following behind the hearse as it heads to a cemetery.

CONTINUED:

FADE TO:

INT. PROVIDENCE APARTMENT - MID AFTERNOON (LATER THAT DAY)

Returning from Randy's funeral, Joe makes his way up the stairs of his apartment building. Getting to the top, he notices some packed boxes and a suitcase in Sarah's open doorway and he knocks to get her attention.

> SARAH
> Wow! Look at you all handsome and dressed up in a suit and tie. Where you going?

> JOE
> Actually, it's where I'm coming from. I attended a funeral this morning.

> SARAH
> Oh... I'm sorry. Was it for that guy Randy that I've been seeing all over the news this week?

> JOE
> Sadly, yes. He was one of my best friends on the planet. I'm going to miss him a lot, but my faith tells me that he is in a much better place than here in Providence, Rhode Island. I guess we all need to go home to God eventually.

> SARAH
> Speaking of going home, thanks to the talk that you and I had, I've decided to head back to Florida. I spoke to my mother, who said that she'd be delighted if I moved back home with her. We forgave each other and she's helping me land a job as a secretary at her office.

> JOE
> Sarah, that is great! I was wondering what the suitcase and boxes were all about. Of course I'll miss seeing you around here, though.

                    SARAH
     I'll miss you, too. Even though we
     didn't get to know each other well, I
     feel like you were an angel sent to
     me so I would change my life.

                    JOE
     That makes me feel very special.
     Thank you... and I hope that you know
     that YOU are a special person.

                    SARAH
     I'm beginning to feel like that,
     thanks.

                    JOE
     So, when do you leave?

                    SARAH
     Pretty much, right now. I was just
     waiting to see you so I could say
     goodbye and thank you.

                    JOE
     Awww...

The two hug.

                                        DISSOLVE TO:

INT. JOE'S APARTMENT ROOM - MOMENTS LATER

Upon entering his apartment, Joe collapses on his bed and
begins to take off his tie. The phone begins to ring, and he
wearily looks over at it before getting up and answering it.

                    JOE
     Hello.

                    RECORD PRODUCER
     Hello, is this Joe?

                    JOE
     Yes it is.

                    RECORD PRODUCER
     This is the record producer that you
     met at The Bitter End.

                    JOE
     Oh, wow. Nice to hear from you.

                                        (CONTINUED)

CONTINUED:

                    RECORD PRODUCER
          I took a listen to your songs, and I
          can tell you that I can't get them
          out of my head.

                    JOE
          Should I take that as a compliment?

                    RECORD PRODUCER
          Absolutely. Your songs are well
          written.

                    JOE
          That means a lot to me. Thank you. Is
          there any chance that you would
          consider producing these songs? You
          can add to them whatever instruments
          and orchestrations that you'd like.

                    RECORD PRODUCER
          We will need to ink out some sort of
          a deal, but yes, I feel that I could
          do a lot with your music.

                    JOE
          This is like a musical dream come
          true for me, considering that I've
          been a fan of yours for many years. I
          do need to tell you that I made a
          promise to record one more song for
          my CD to benefit St. Jude's
          Children's Hospital in Memphis. Would
          that be OK with you?

                    RECORD PRODUCER
          I don't see why not. We could record
          it together at my studio in the
          Hamptons. Do you have a specific song
          in mind?

                    JOE
          That would be fun! Yes, I think I'd
          like to do a cover of David Bowie's
          'Starman'.
                    (MORE)

CONTINUED:

                    JOE (cont'd)
          I've always liked that song, and I
          think the lyrics are perfect for a
          children's hospital charity:
          "Let the children use it...
          Let the children lose it...
          Let all the children boogie..."
          In this case, those lyrics in the
          chorus represent the children using
          funds from the song to help combat
          their illness, losing the illness,
          and then dancing and living again.

                    RECORD PRODUCER
          Perfect. Let me look at my schedule
          and I will get back in touch with you
          to set up the session.

                                        FADE TO:

INT. PRODUCER'S RECORDING STUDIO - MORNING (2 WEEKS LATER)

Joe is siting behind a drum set, while the producer paces
back and forth in front of the drums with headphones on.

                    RECORD PRODUCER
          OK. Take it again from the top.

Also wearing headphones, Joe begins to play the drum parts
of the song while the producer listens intently. This scene
also includes cut-aways to Joe recording acoustic guitar and
then to him singing some vocals into a specialized
microphone. The on-screen scene includes the superimposed
hands of a clock spinning around, denoting that the day was
dedicated to meticulously recording the song. Intertwined
with this scene are cutaways to the producer at a mixing
board console saying things like "Let's re-do that", "Again,
from the top", "Not bad, but I know you can do better"...

                                        DISSOLVE TO:

EXT. OUTSIDE DECK AT PRODUCER'S HOUSE - EARLY EVENING

The producer is flipping burgers on the grill while Joe sips
on a beer as he overlooks the Atlantic Ocean from the
second-floor wrap-around wooden deck at the producer's
house.

                    JOE
          This place is amazing. What a
          beautiful view.

                                        (CONTINUED)

CONTINUED:

> RECORD PRODUCER
> Thanks. Yeah, we love it here. It is
> such a nice change from the city. I
> hope that you don't mind veggie
> burgers.

> JOE
> Sounds great to me. Thanks for
> grilling.

> RECORD PRODUCER
> My pleasure. I want to mention that I
> know you look up to me for the
> musical work that I've done over the
> years, but I want you to know that
> I'm a fan of yours.

> JOE
> What do you mean?

> RECORD PRODUCER
> I mean that you're a terrific
> drummer, yet can also play guitar,
> piano, sing, and write really good
> songs. I admire that.

> JOE
> You have no idea how much your words
> mean to me. To be a musician and have
> my musical idol say words like that
> is mind-blowing to me. I feel like I
> finally made it.

> RECORD PRODUCER
> You should feel good about what you
> do. You've obviously worked hard at
> your craft.

> JOE
> Thank you... and speaking of working
> hard, I know that you will be putting
> in a lot of effort on this record and
> I want to give back. The wood on this
> deck seems like it has seen its share
> of the elements. When was the last
> time it was treated with waterproof
> stain?

> RECORD PRODUCER
> I'm not sure that it was ever treated
> since we've owned the house.

CONTINUED:

> JOE
> Then allow me to come back in a week
> or two to stain the deck as a thank
> you for all that you are doing for
> this record.

> RECORD PRODUCER
> Really? This is a very large deck.

> JOE
> It would be a small effort compared
> to everything that you are doing for
> me.

DISSOLVE TO:

EXT. OUTSIDE DECK AT PRODUCER'S HOUSE - 2 WEEKS LATER

The sun is beating down on Joe's neck as his paint brush of
deck stain glides over board after thirsty board of the
massive deck. He hears the gate open at the end of the
driveway, and the record producer's car pulls in. Joe pauses
for a moment and watches him get out of the car.

> RECORD PRODUCER
> Hey Joe, how is it going up there?

> JOE
> So far so good. I think that you're
> going to like the color of this
> stain. It is making the wood look
> brand new again.

The producer opens up the trunk of his car, pulls out a
large boom-box CD player, and sets it on the roof of his
car.

> RECORD PRODUCER
> I've got great news. Will from the
> Late Show added bass to 'Starman',
> and Ace Frehley of the band KISS
> recorded a lead guitar part on it.
> Listen to this!

The producer hits play on the boom-box then leans back
against his car. Joe places his brush on the can of deck
stain, leans over the railing of the deck, and shakes his
head in amazement that not only is his drummer hero
producing his record, but the guitar hero from his favorite
band growing up is playing guitar on his recording.

<PLAY SONG 'STARMAN'>

CONTINUED:

FADE TO:

INT. JOE'S HOUSE - ONE YEAR LATER

Sitting on his bed, Joe has an acoustic guitar in his lap that he is leaning over to write some lyrics onto a notebook page. The phone rings and he hesitates to answer it while finishing writing down the line of the song. He finally lays the guitar on top of the bed then rushes to answer the phone. Joe picks up the receiver at the same time that the answering machine turns on, causing communication confusion between the caller and Joe.

                    JOE
          Hello...

                    ANSWERING MACHINE
          Hi. This is Joe...

                    JOE
          Shoot! Hang on...

                    ANSWERING MACHINE
          Unfortunately, I am unable to answer
          the phone at this time...

                    JOE
          No! I'm here...

                    ANSWERING MACHINE
          Please leave a message after the
          tone...

                    JOE
          Ugh!

                    ANSWERING MACHINE
          BEEP!

                    LENNY
               (off screen)
          Um... Joe?

                    JOE
          Lenny! I am sorry for the confusion.
          Got to the phone too late.

                    LENNY
               (off screen)
          When the heck are you going to get a
          new phone? You know that they have
          mobile phones now, right?

(CONTINUED)

CONTINUED:

                    JOE
          Yeah, I was thinking about getting
          one. How are you?

                    LENNY
               (off screen)
          Things are rocking and rolling for me
          out here in L.A., and I know that
          they are for you, too... I've been
          hearing some of your songs on the
          radio!

                    JOE
          Yeah! Finally, things are beginning
          to happen! I've been told that a full
          tour is being booked. I'll begin
          rehearsals soon.

                    LENNY
               (off screen)
          Yes, that is quite exciting. You've
          been working hard at this and nobody
          can say that you haven't paid your
          dues, and then some!

                    JOE
          Thanks Lenny... That means a lot
          coming from you.

                    LENNY
               (off screen)
          Don't thank me yet, but you can thank
          me after I tell you this. Consider
          the kick-off to your tour happening
          at Fenway Park.

                    JOE
          What do you mean?

                    LENNY
               (off screen)
          I mean, YOU stepping up to home plate
          and singing the National Anthem to
          40,000 Red Sox fans before a game
          next month.

                    JOE
          Lenny, are you serious?

CONTINUED:

                         LENNY
                      (off screen)
          I've known you a long time, and know
          how badly you've wanted to go to bat
          as a player for the Boston Red Sox.
          Now you can stand at that plate and
          belt out the anthem right over the
          Green Monster wall in left field! You
          are already booked, and the Red Sox
          team and managers are looking forward
          to hosting you...

                                      DISSOLVE TO:

EXT. FENWAY PARK IN BOSTON - EARLY EVENING

Fenway Park is packed with 40,000 baseball fans. The Boston
Red Sox players are being introduced over the historic ball
park's speakers, as each one stands along the first-base
line during pre-game ceremonies. Joe is standing near home
plate with his acoustic guitar, where a newspaper reporter
is asking him questions.

                    NEWSPAPER REPORTER
          Here we are, minutes before you are
          to sing the National Anthem at the
          highest-attended game on record here
          at Fenway Park. How nervous are you?

Joe looks down and scuffs the dirt surrounding home plate a
little bit, like a batter would, but with his black cowboy
boots instead of cleats, before answering the question.

                         JOE
          You know, I hadn't thought about
          that, but now that you've asked I can
          say that I am not nervous at all. I
          kind of wish I was so I could feel
          the moment even that much more
          intensely... But I can tell you that
          this is a thrill of a lifetime for
          me.

Joe pulls a photo of his grandfather out of his pocket and
shows it to the reporter.

                    JOE (cont'd)
          I will be thinking of this guy the
          entire time I sing the anthem. That's
          my grandfather, who would take me to
          one game here every summer when I was
          young.
                       (MORE)

                                      (CONTINUED)

CONTINUED:

>   JOE (cont'd)
>   I would promise him each and every
>   time that one day I would be stepping
>   up to this plate. I just didn't know
>   that it would be as a singer and not
>   a baseball player, but I am making
>   good on my promise to him tonight.

The reporter is writing down all of Joe's words.

>   NEWSPAPER REPORTER
>   Wow! That's a great story.

A sound technician with the Boston Red Sox organization
walks up to Joe with two microphone stands and instructs him
to follow. Joe hands the photo of his grandfather to the
reporter.

>   JOE
>   I need to get ready to sing now.
>   Would you mind holding this photo
>   until I am done?

>   NEWSPAPER REPORTER
>   I don't mind at all. We can finish
>   the interview after the anthem.

Joe begins to follow the Red Sox technician with the
microphone stands, looks back, then quickly returns to the
reporter.

>   JOE
>   I'm sorry, but would you mind holding
>   the photo such that my grandfather's
>   image is facing me?

>   NEWSPAPER REPORTER
>   I think that's a great idea!

Scurrying back to the place on the field where the
microphones are set-up, Joe realizes that the vocal stand
keeps wobbling due to the thickness of the ball field grass
that it is stationed upon, just as the announcer begins to
ask the mass of people packed inside the stadium to rise to
their feet.

STADIUM LOUDSPEAKERS:

"Ladies and Gentlemen... Please rise for our National
Anthem. It is being sung by Rhode Island native, Joe Silva,
who is a Sun Studio Recording Artist."

Joe re-positions one of the microphone stand once more then
begins to strum his guitar.

(CONTINUED)

CONTINUED:

He hears his playing return to his ears from the sound
system a full second after he strums his guitar, due to the
vastness of the stadium. After a few strums, he begins to
sing into the vocal microphone. Unfortunately, no vocal
sound is returning to Joe's ears, or the ears of anyone
else, from the sound system. It becomes apparent that the
microphone isn't working for some reason. He stops strumming
his guitar and calls over the technician, signaling that the
microphone isn't working. The crowd begins to cheer in
support as the technician works on the microphone. Soon, the
technician runs away from the microphone and Joe speaks into
it...

                    JOE
          Test... 1... 2...

Joe hears his voice return from Fenway Park's sound-system,
as the crowd erupts. He begins to strum his guitar once more
and delivers the National Anthem to Red Sox Nation, which
is 40,000 strong in the stadium. As he gets to the end of
the song, he strums the last chord and is amazed at the
audible-level of the audience cheering. Joe looks up to the
sky, briefly places his right hand on his heart, then
quickly raises it toward Heaven in a salute of gratitude to
God, and his grandfather, before stepping away from the
microphones and returning to the reporter.

                    NEWSPAPER REPORTER
          That was amazing... How did it feel
          to sing our nation's anthem to forty-
          thousand people?

The reporter returns to Joe the photo of his grandfather.
Joe accepts it and hold it against his heart, while his
guitar still dangles just below his chest.

                    JOE
          Well, scratch what I said about not
          being nervous. When the microphone
          didn't work initially, I finally felt
          nervous... VERY nervous! I didn't
          want to strike-out at my only "up-to-
          bat", if you will.

                    NEWSPAPER REPORTER
          May I print that?

                    JOE
          Of course! It is best to keep
          everything real. Newspapers have made
          a big impact on my life.

                              FADE TO:

INT./EXT. INSIDE LIMOUSINE - EARLY EVENING LOS ANGELES (5 MONTHS LATER)

Riding down Coldwater Canyon Avenue, Joe is sitting up front with the chauffeur, pointing out personal landmarks along the way.

                    JOE
          That building up on the left is where
          my apartment was. There is a gas
          station market just on the other side
          of it that I'd like you to pull into
          please, Jean-Claude.

The limousine pulls along-side of a fence on the outskirt of the gas station. Joe gets out and walks into the Mini-Mart building at the station, carrying an envelope.

INSIDE MINI MART AT COUNTER

Joe begins speaking to the clerk behind the counter.

                    JOE (cont'd)
          Hello. Sorry to bother you, but I'm
          wondering if One Eye Don still comes
          around here in the evening?

                    MINI-MART CLERK
          I am sorry, my friend, but he is
          usually here in the morning, filling
          up his truck with gas on the way to
          his work.

Joe's face lights up with a huge smile.

                    JOE
          I am SO happy to hear that. Thank you
          very much, sir.

Returning to the front seat of the limousine, Joe points out the direction in which he'd like the chauffeur, Jean-Claude, to drive. The scene then shows the limo pulling up in front of the Little Brown Church. Joe lets himself out of the front passenger-side of the vehicle, still holding onto the envelope, and enters the church while Jean-Claude gets out and waits near the back door of the limousine.

                                        DISSOLVE TO:

Jean-Claude opens the back door of the limousine. Joe places the envelope in a donation box as he exits the Little Brown Church.

                                        (CONTINUED)

CONTINUED:

He nods to Jean-Claude as he gets into the back of the
limousine, joining Donny, who is already seated in the limo,
handing Joe a beer as he sits down.

                    DONNY
          Who else is doing this?

The two clink their bottles in celebration. A radio disc-
jockey is now audible in this scene.

                    RADIO DISC JOCKEY
          With a tour rolling into Hollywood
          tonight, this is Joe's latest
          single...

<PLAY SONG 'FOREVER THERE FOR YOU' RADIO VERSION>

                                        DISSOLVE TO:

EXT. HELIPORT / AIRPORT - MOMENTS LATER

The sound of of helicopter blades is apparent at first,
blending with the music as the image is that of Joe's boots
walking atop a tarmac. The camera pans back and away to see
the full image of Joe and Donny making their way to, and
then into, a helicopter. Donny takes a back seat while Joe
sits up front with the pilot. The helicopter lifts into the
air, higher and higher, granting a panoramic view of the San
Fernando Valley before heading toward the Hollywood Hills.
Joe reaches for his wallet and pulls out a photo of his
sister Jade, and his friend Randy. In doing so, a photo of
Shelly falls out of his wallet and onto the floor of the
helicopter as they pass over the Hollywood Bowl Overlook.
Joe looks at the photo of Shelly and decides to leave it
there at his feet as he positions the pictures of Jade and
Randy in his hand such that they are looking out the window.
The helicopter circles above the Hollywood Bowl a few times
so Joe and Donny can get a good look at the gathering crowd
for tonight's concert, then heads out toward the horizon for
several miles after passing the tall buildings that comprise
downtown Los Angeles. Eventually, the pilot banks the
helicopter toward the shoreline until they are over Venice
Beach and the Santa Monica Pier. Joe peers out over the
coast, then down at the photo of Shelly at his feet. He
hears Randy's voice in his head while visually recalling
moments that he shared with Shelly on Venice Beach and the
Santa Monica Pier...

(Randy's Voice)
"You know how to make it less painful? Walk right up to both
of them, say hello to Shelly and hold out your hand to the
new guy. Shake his hand and introduce yourself.

                                        (CONTINUED)

CONTINUED:

You'll be surprised at what forgiveness can do. Plus, you'll leave a good reputation in your wake."

The helicopter swoops away from the coast and heads toward the uniquely round Capitol Records building. Joe gets a mental flashback of running into that building with his band's promotional packages while Shelly waited outside for him, and he hears the voice of One Eye Don in his head...

(One Eye Don's Voice)
"I'll give you one last bit of advice, Joe. Forgive her. You won't truly heal or move on until you do. I've forgiven everyone from my past, including my father, and whoever stole all of my tools, equipment, and pick-up truck. I have felt better ever since."

Joe reaches down near his feet, picks up the photo of Shelly, and stares at it for a moment. Soon, he smiles, presses it to his heart, then adds it to the other two photos that are facing out the window. With a look of relief and sudden peacefulness, he signals the pilot to make one more swing above Los Angeles.

DISSOLVE TO:

The helicopter eventually lands atop the Hollywood Bowl Overlook. Joe and Donny exit the helicopter and jump into the waiting limousine. The scene then shows the limousine pulling away with a police escort, on the way to Joe's concert at the Hollywood Bowl (the song 'Forever There for You' is still playing throughout this scene).

DISSOLVE TO:

INSIDE LIMOUSINE

The escorted limo winds its way down the Hollywood Hills, as Joe reaches for his ringing cell phone.

                    JOE
          Hello...

                    JOE'S FATHER
          What do you figure, Joe?

                    JOE
          Hi Dad! SUCCESS!!!

DISSOLVE TO:

The limousine follows the police escort as it pulls into the venue, passing the Hollywood Bowl sign.

CONTINUED:

DISSOLVE TO:

EXT. HOLLYWOOD BOWL STAGE - EVENING

As the song 'Forever There for You' nears its end, the scene shows Joe and his live band performing it on the Hollywood Bowl stage. The audience is on its feet, singing along until the song's end. Joe then addresses the audience before performing his final song of the concert.

> JOE
> Thank you all so very much for being here tonight. I can't tell you how much it means to me. Standing here on this stage and performing for you all this evening has been a dream of mine for most of my life, and it has been quite the journey to get here. During that journey, I've learned a lot about myself, and a lot about living. There are several people that I've met along the way to whom I owe my fullest gratitude, for each of them gave me a valuable lesson that were necessary pieces of the overall puzzle of my dream, and more importantly, my life. What I have realized is that my dream was BEING realized during each and every day of my journey, including my many days of struggle, for it was during those days that my strength was building, my character was growing, and my appreciation of better days was being developed. The one lesson that has helped me the most was the lesson on forgiveness. I've known that granting genuine forgiveness is one of the hardest things to do in life, but I've come to learn that forgiveness is what allows the negativity and weight of the world to be released from one's shoulders, allowing the person to finally soar to the heights of their dreams... This last song that we will perform for you is all about forgiveness... It is called 'Let It Go'.

<PLAY SONG 'LET IT GO'>

(CONTINUED)

CONTINUED:

This scene shows Joe and the band perform the full song in concert. The audience's vocal participation grows with each chorus until the entire body of people in attendance is singing along by the end of the song. At one point, we see Joe's former room-mate and keyboardist Jeff onstage playing the tambourine, and Joe walking over to him and embracing with a hug. As the song ends, and the audience is cheering while Joe makes his way to both sides of the stage to wave farewell to his audience, a tan hat with an over-sized brim is thrown onto the stage from the crowd. Joe reaches down and picks it up before looking out to see who might have thrown it onto the stage. As he places it on his head to allow the brim to shade his eyes from the spotlight, Joe notices a man that is undoubtedly One-Eye-Don walking up the isle away from the stage, while the rest of the several thousand people are still cheering and facing the stage. With a quick glance back, One-Eye-Don gives a thumbs-up to Joe. Removing the hat from its position of shadowing his vision from the spotlight, Joe holds the hat to his heart in a gesture toward One-Eye-Don, then looking up, past the spotlights, Joe waves the hat high up into the air as a gesture toward Heaven...

FADE TO BLACK

CONTINUED:

CONTINUED:

From The Author...

Thank you for taking time to experience 'A Journey Through A Dream'. This literary and musical work is based on a true story - my story. Some venues and people names have been changed to fit the script, and certain characters are a combination of a few real-life people that became one person (for instance, the character JADE is a combination of my real-life sisters Jane and Jude... Mr. Durago is a combination of my school music teachers, Mr. Durand and Mr. Aragao). The sequence of events have been slightly altered to keep the story flowing in a movie format, but most of the scenes have actually happened to me in one form or another... all but the very last Hollywood Bowl scene. I have performed in venues larger than the Hollywood Bowl, but playing the Bowl has always been an early dream of mine. It is the dream that I keep inside my pocket, which has given me so many dream-come-true moments throughout my life as I fervently pursue my goal of stepping onto the Hollywood Bowl stage.

My actual journey includes at least a thousand more characters and scenes than those that have been depicted in 'A Journey Through A Dream'. While I penned this script, I was reminded of how the actual journey toward any given dream is the real reward gained while reaching for one's dream-based goals... For me, my rewards came in the form of performing on tour-dates with over 40 of my musical heroes, such as: B.B. King, The Beach Boys, The Alarm, Joan Jett, and so many others, playing concerts in seven countries... those rewards came every time I stepped into recording studios like Abbey Road or Sun Studio to give birth to my songs... and some of the best rewards over all were found in all of the very special people that I've met along my path.

Though there have been many rewards, my journey also included several scenes that were not very pleasant to live through, but in looking back and reflecting upon them, I realize how they were very necessary for the growth of my human self, and even more importantly, for my soul's development. I do hope that each reader receives the many messages and lessons that are intertwined throughout the journey... not only mine, but the personal journey that each reader is currently on in life. It is my belief that human beings learn important lessons every day of their lives.

All too often, we as people tend to live in the future as we work on pushing our dreams and goals toward the peak of the hill while ignoring the beauty that each present moment surrounds us with. Having achieved many of my dreams in life, I now ponder the long path that brought me to where I am today, or rather the road that I paved with my two bare hands while God helped to clear the way in front of me.

(CONTINUED)

CONTINUED:

I subscribe to the notion that God helps those that help themselves, and as I look back at all of those decades during which I laughed and cried, bled and healed, loved - lost - and then loved again, gave and received, sacrificed and often risked everything, I realize again that the true reward was there all along - the actual journey toward my dream - traveling at the speed of life. My personal journey has been so long that if it could be measured in miles I'd surely be a citizen martian by now.

I dedicate 'A Journey Through A Dream' to all of my family and friends who have helped me along my path on earth. Truly, I hope that I have somehow helped you all, too, and served you with an abundance of love.

To my children, I hope that you never get to a point in life where you feel that you have hit rock-bottom, but I do wish that you are blessed with all of the lessons that come from experiencing the lowest of points in life.

I sincerely send a heart-felt thank you to ALL of you, and send a special nod of gratitude to the cast and crew of 'Married... with Children', who took me under their wings and kept me fed when I was hungry and made sure that I remained alive when I became desperate... To 'One-Eye-Don', the homeless man who saved my life one fateful December night in Los Angeles, I will never forget you or the wisdom that you gave to me... To Randy Hien who gave me my first show as an original performer and believed in me since day one, I feel your Omni-present effect on my life as I recount the hundreds of lessons and opportunities that you've bestowed upon me. Undoubtedly, I have learned that angels do walk among us and guide us through life.

May this story help everyone realize that we shouldn't judge each other by what we only see on the surface, but rather that we should show each other compassion, forgiveness and love, while somehow assisting and serving each other through life. One never knows whose eyes, or eye, God is looking through.

Joe Silva

(CONTINUED)

CONTINUED:

CONTINUED:

CONTINUED:

THANK YOU...

God, my Parents and Siblings, Lynn, Jude, Jane, Lisa,
my Children Charline and Tyler,
Anton Fig, Will Lee,
Jim McCarthy, Dean Landry, David Gaspar, Don Platt,
Mike Savard, Thom Keough,
Steven Ritt, Victor Aragao, Bill Durand, Nectar Lennox,
Patty and Loren Harriet, Ace Frehley, Bruce Davenport,
Randy Hien,
Phebe and Keith Wheeler, John Conti,
Scott Diodati, Marjorie and Alan Freedman,
Nancy Priddy, Christina Applegate, Martyn LeNoble,
Taylor Hawkins and Everyone in the Foo Fighters' camp,
David Vierra, Mike Giangreco, Jan and Kevin Keough,
John Pomfret, Marc and Michael Harris,
Rock & Roll Pizza Moorpark, Pig-N-Whistle Hollywood,
The Living Room in Providence, RI,
The Parlour, The Hien Family, Gregory Rourke,
Melanie Athena, The McCarthy Family, The Landry Family,
Evel Knievel, B.B.King,
James Lott, Billy Swan,
Jimmy Tittle, Kathy Cash,
Mike Kelley, Carl Reed, Mike DiPietro,
Betty and Carl Costa, Melanie and Joe Lameiras,
Colleen Rose and Ken Novak,
Lupo's Heartbreak Hotel, Carol and Tom Ward,
Bob Cowsill, Andi Lee, James Stevenson,
The Alarm, Jules and Mike Peters,
Andy Lebrow, Craig Adams, Dave Clarke, Dave Francis,
Gary Twinn, Graham Leigh, JJ Haggar,
Joff Northfield, Lydia Franklin, Mark Warden,
Rob Hurst, Ro Ashika, Warren Curtis,
Tour Bus Live, Jim Paon, Dave Amadio,
Mike Farrell, Bert Cook, Vicki Abelson,
Clem Burke, Gregg Bissonette,
Sian Llewellyn, Gavin Martin, Simon Hardeman, Dave Everley,
Dr. Charles, The Boston Red Sox,
Mario Pregoni, BBC Radio Wales, Alan Thompson,
Hard Rock Cafe Dublin, Kip Winger, Lisa Lindberg,
Amy Nachbar, Sandi LaPlace, Joe Medeiros,
One Eye Don,
Brian "Birdman" Schofield, Kristin Anderson,
Aynsley Dunbar, The Bitter End NYC, The Montegu Family,
Baggot Inn Dublin, Radio Nova Ireland,
94WHJY Providence,
Cheryl Harvey, Rick MacKenzie, WAAF Radio Worcester,
Jason Kornberg, The Hooters, Missing Persons, Joe Satriani,
The Beach Boys, Ringo Starr, Billy Squier,
Henry Lee Summer, Concrete Blonde, Robin Trower,
The Payolas, Cheap Trick, KISS,
Mark Baxter, Bob Guisti, Stephen Pellegrino,
Jimmy Olson, Cory Pesaturo, Lori Luther,

(CONTINUED)

CONTINUED:

Joan Jett, Michael Turco, Marguerite Hibbets,
Sue Therien, Luke Gaskell, Ricardo Alves,
Christian Brooks,
Patricia and Christian DeFrancesco, Michelle Fletcher,
Owen Korb, Linda Stanley, Laura Dvorak, Barbera Bellagamba,
Uliana Salerno, Nese Eddleman, Anne-Cecile Bedford,
John Kaminski, Lauren Noble, Cathy and Chris Waugh,
Jacqueline Gormley, George Lallier, Peter Radin,
Dale Mumford, Edward Mitsmenn, Colleen Pinelli,
Johanna MacDonald, Maryann Seebeck, ,Dennis Verduchi
Kevin Sittinger, Robert Tetreault, Michael Botts,
Peter Tork (The Monkees), Leslie West,
Garland Jeffreys, Escape Club,
Kevin Falvey,
Journey / The Storm,
Mark Teixeira, Marty Ballou,
The Schemers, The Neighborhoods,
Extreme, Quiet Riot,
Corey Glover / Living Colour,
Howard Devoto / Buzzcocks,
Joe Strummer / The Clash,
Cha-Chi Loprette, WBCN Boston,
Sun Studio,
Danny Coleman, Chevy Metal Band, Oz Noy,
John Mailloux / Bongo Beach Productions,
Ida Langsam, The Call, International Swingers,
Late Show with David Letterman,
Brian Mitchell, The Ramones,
Jo Borozny-Yeule / The Garage,
Jim Sykes / Elvis Radio,
Peter Pomfret, Chris Gasbarro, Jim Paon,
Colleen Curtis, Edward Fernald, Izzy Presley,
Greg Bass, Judith and Ernie Potter,
Abbey Road Studios,
606 Studio,
Aleksandr Krepkikh,
Lion Head Studio,
The Daily Mail U.K.,
Classic Rock Magazine,
Irene and Dan Meleleu, Pat Clancy,
Kimbery Doyle, Mark Sawaia,
Radio Albatross U.K.,
BBC Radio Darby,
and 1,000 more of you who have helped me along my journey...
Much love and gratitude to ALL of you.

(CONTINUED)

CONTINUED:

SONG LYRICS

EGYPTIAN LOVE SONG
Lyrics by: Joe Silva   Music by: Joe Silva & David Gaspar

CHILDREN OF EGYPT - RICH AND POOR - LIVING IN THE DESERT
YOUR DADDY SAT HIGH UPON A THRONE ONE DAY YOU WOULD INHERIT
THERE WERE KINGS AND THERE WERE SLAVES AND THERE WAS US
THERE WERE TREASURES UNDER TRIANGLE ROCKS
FOR WHEN YOU TURN TO DUST
MATERIAL THINGS I HAVE ARE FEW - FOREVER I'LL SING TO YOU

EGYPTIAN LOVE SONGS

BROTHER AND SISTER - KING AND QUEEN - RULING IN THE DESERT
AFTER THREE SHORT YEARS PTOLEMY WANTS TO MAKE THE QUEEN A
PEASANT
SO YOU PROMPTLY GATHERED AN ARMY IN SYRIA
BUT COULD NEVER MAKE GOOD OF YOUR CLAIM
BY FORCING WAR
JULIUS CAME TO YOUR RESCUE - FOREVER I'LL SING TO YOU

EGYPTIAN LOVE SONGS

JULIUS CAME AND WENT FROM YOU - BUT STILL I'LL SING TO YOU

EGYPTIAN LOVE SONGS

REMEMBER HOW WHEN WE WERE SO YOUNG YOU FELL INTO MY ARMS
BUT YOU MET MARK ANTHONY WHO HAD A WIFE BUT FELL TO YOUR
CHARMS
HE HAD TO GO AND DIE IN THE WAR OF HIS WIFE
A BITE FROM A SNAKE IS ALL IT TOOK TO TAKE YOUR LIFE
SO MANY THINGS I WANTED TO SAY TO YOU - FOREVER I'LL SING TO
YOU

EGYPTIAN LOVE SONGS

CONTINUED:

I'D BLEED
Lyrics by: Joe Silva Music by: Joe Silva & Carl Costa

HAVE YOU SEEN THE SEVEN WONDERS
I SEE THE EIGHTH ONE WHEN I LOOK AT YOU
HAVE YOU HEARD THE WORDS I BLUNDER
WHEN I SAY I LOVE YOU - DO YOU LOVE ME TOO

IF I NEVER GET THE CHANCE TO SAY AGAIN
HOW BEAUTIFUL YOUR SOUL HAS ALWAYS BEEN
I'D BLEED

CAN YOU TASTE THIS EVERLASTING FLAVOR
OF LOVE THAT LASTS FOREVER
MY KISS OF LOVE IS TRUE
CAN YOU FEEL HOW DEEP MY LOVE RUNS
WHEN YOU AND I BECOME ONE - IT'S LIKE A LIFE BRAND NEW

IF I NEVER GET THE CHANCE TO SAY AGAIN
HOW BEAUTIFUL YOUR SOUL HAS ALWAYS BEEN
I'D BLEED

I WOULDN'T BREATHE IF I CAN'T FIND YOU
DON'T WANT TO SMELL YOUR PERFUME ON SOMEONE NEW

IF I NEVER HAVE THE CHANCE TO SAY AGAIN
HOW BEAUTIFUL YOUR SOUL HAS ALWAYS BEEN
IF I NEVER GET THE CHANCE TO SAY AGAIN
HOW BEAUTIFUL YOUR SOUL HAS ALWAYS BEEN

I'D BLEED MY SENSES DRY

CONTINUED:

MY TODAY MY TOMORROW
Lyrics & Music by: Joe Silva

I COULD NEVER TELL YOU WHAT IT MEANS TO HOLD YOU
MY LOVE FOR YOU IS MORE THAN ANY WORDS CAN SAY
BUT YOU CAN SEE MY HANDS SHAKE
CAN'T YOU TELL THAT I'M TALKING FUNNY
KISS ME ONE MORE TIME AND TAKE MY BREATH AWAY
'CAUSE I DON'T REALLY WANT TO BE WITH ANYONE ELSE TONIGHT
YOU'RE ALL THAT I THINK OF - ALL THAT I NEED
SO BE MY BABE

(Chorus)
BE MY TODAY BE MY TOMORROW
BE MY LIFE SO I CAN THINK AGAIN
I'M OUT OF SORTS WITHOUT YOU - I MISS YOU
BE MY TODAY BE MY TOMORROW
BE MY LIFE SO I CAN BE ME AGAIN
I'M OUT OF SORTS WITHOUT YOU

HOW IT FEELS TO NEED YOU - HOURS FEEL LIKE DAYS WITHOUT YOU
SAY YOU'LL MEET ME ON THE MOON AND I'LL BE THERE
THE PHONE ACROSS THE HALL RINGS
I WILL PICK IT UP IN JUST A MINUTE
I'VE GOT TO MAKE A WISH THAT IT'S YOUR VOICE I HEAR
'CAUSE I DON'T REALLY WANT TO TALK TO ANYONE ELSE TONIGHT
YOU'RE ALL THAT I THINK OF - ALL THAT I NEED
SO BE MY BABE

(Chorus)

I'VE BEEN AROUND THIS WORLD
SAW EVERYTHING THAT I COULD SEE
I BELIEVE IN GOD - OH I BELIEVE IN YOU WITH ME

I DON'T REALLY WANT TO GO WITH ANYONE ELSE TONIGHT
YOU'RE ALL THAT I THINK OF - ALL THAT I NEED
SO BE MY BABE

(Chorus)

(CONTINUED)

CONTINUED:

JUST YOU AND...
Lyrics & Music by: Joe Silva

HAS IT FALLEN - POSSIBLY
BUT IT FEELS SO VERY STRANGE TO ME
LIKE THE FIRST TIME IN A LONG TIME GOOD
YET THE KNOWING YOU'RE THE LAST TO BLEED
IS THERE A WORD INSENSITY
FOR IT SOUNDS A LITTLE STRANGE TO ME
LIKE A WILD-FIRE TO CHANGE THE WORLD FOR GOOD
OR A BLAZE SET TO SET ONE FREE

I KNOW I SHOULD FORGET TO WRITE THIS DOWN
I'LL ONLY SAY IT IN MY DREAMS
IF YOU HEAR IT THEN YOU'LL KNOW THAT IT WAS MEANT TO BE
JUST YOU AND...

POSSIBLY - BUT COULD YOU PLEASE EXPLAIN TO ME
WHY I'VE KNOWN IT CLEARLY FOR A LONG LONG TIME
YET A MYSTERY I STILL CAN'T SEE

I KNOW I SHOULD FORGET TO WRITE THIS DOWN
I'LL ONLY SAY IT IN MY DREAMS
IF YOU HEAR IT THEN YOU'LL KNOW THAT IT WAS MEANT TO BE
JUST YOU AND...

HONESTLY - MAYBE LOVE IS JUST A LUXURY
SMART ENOUGH TO BUILD A CASTLE GOOD
YET FOOL ENOUGH TO LOSE THE KEY

I KNOW I SHOULD FORGET TO WRITE THIS DOWN
I'LL ONLY SAY IT IN MY DREAMS
IF YOU HEAR IT THEN YOU'LL KNOW THAT IT WAS MEANT TO BE
JUST YOU AND...

(CONTINUED)

CONTINUED:

CHANGING
Lyrics & Music by: Joe Silva

I NEVER MEANT TO MAKE YOU CRY
I WANT TO DRINK THAT TEAR
AND POUR THE LOVE BACK IN YOUR EYES
THINK OF DAYS OUR LOVE WAS YOUNG
COULD YOU FORGET THE WORDS TO EVERY SONG WE SUNG
I START BREAKING DOWN WHEN
FRIENDS ASK ME WHERE'S YOUR BETTER HALF BEEN
WITHOUT YOU I'M A PLANE WITHOUT WINGS - I'M CRASHING

STOP ME FROM BELIEVING - WE'RE CHANGING LIKE THE SEASONS
WINTER SPRING AND SUMMER
BUT DON'T FALL OUT OF LOVE

HOW CAN ANOTHER GIRL TAKE YOUR PLACE
WHEN EVERY TIME I CLOSE MY EYES I ONLY SEE YOUR FACE
I'LL KEEP MY THOUGHTS LOCKED IN A JAR
MY THOUGHTS RUN OUT OF MY MIND - THEY SOMETIMES RUN TOO FAR
I HAD A TERRIBLE DREAM AND I WOKE UP - I WAS BELIEVING
YOU WERE FALLING IN LOVE WITH ANOTHER

STOP ME FROM BELIEVING - WE'RE CHANGING LIKE THE SEASONS
WINTER SPRING AND SUMMER
BUT DON'T FALL OUT OF LOVE WITH ME

CONTINUED:

THE COLDEST DAY OF THE YEAR
Lyrics & Music by: Joe Silva

YOU SAID HAPPY BIRTHDAY - I'LL MISS YOU - GOODBYE
THEN YOU WENT AWAY IN THE MORNING
I WAITED TWO WEEKS FOR A CALL
THEN ON THE DAY THAT YOU PLANNED TO COME HOME
YOUR PHONE CALL WAS A SHOT WITHOUT WARNING
IT DIDN'T SOUND LIKE YOU AT ALL
YOU SAID YOU'VE CHANGED AND THAT YOU'RE HAPPY NOW
THEN YOU CUT MY FEELINGS ON A BROKEN VOW

THE COLDEST DAY OF THE YEAR CAME IN JUNE THIS TIME
MY HEART LAYS FROZEN ON THE CELLAR FLOOR
ON THE COLDEST DAY OF THE YEAR I FELT MY SPIRIT DIE
WHEN YOU SAID YOU DON'T NEED ME ANYMORE
THE PAIN NEVER THAWS

YOU THROW AWAY YEARS LIKE THEY'RE MINUTES TO SPARE
WHEN YOU TOOK HIS HAND WAS IT LIKE YOU
CHOSE A BOOK 'CAUSE THE COVER WAS NEW
WELL THINK ABOUT THIS AS YOU TURN EVERY PAGE
I WISH YOU HAPPILY FOREVER AFTER - BUT STILL
NEW BOOKS GET DUSTY TOO
THOUGH IT SEEMED A SONG COULD FILL MY TIME
WITHOUT YOU THERE'S NO MELODY - THERE'S NO RHYME

SINCE THE COLDEST DAY OF THE YEAR CAME IN JUNE THIS TIME
MY HEART LAYS FROZEN ON THE CELLAR FLOOR
ON THE COLDEST DAY OF THE YEAR I FELT MY SPIRIT DIE
WHEN YOU SAID YOU DON'T NEED ME ANYMORE
THE PAIN NEVER THAWS

MY YEARS WITH YOU - I COULDN'T ASK FOR BETTER DAYS
BUT GOD GIVES AND THEN GOD TAKES AWAY

ON THE COLDEST DAY OF THE YEAR - IT CAME IN JUNE THIS TIME
MY HEART LAYS FROZEN ON THE CELLAR FLOOR
ON THE COLDEST DAY OF THE YEAR I FELT MY SPIRIT DIE
WHEN YOU SAID YOU DON'T NEED ME ANYMORE

(CONTINUED)

CONTINUED:

FOREVER THERE FOR YOU
Lyrics & Music by: Joe Silva

WHEN YOU LEFT YOU LEFT ME GUESSING
AND I GUESS I WAS A BIT CONFUSED
'CAUSE YOU SAID YOU'D NEVER LEAVE ME
THEN YOU LEFT - YOU WENT AWAY TOO SOON
I SUPPOSE I'M BEING SELFISH
SO GOOD LUCK TO YOU WITH WHAT YOU DO
REMEMBER AS YOU START TO DRIFT AWAY FROM ME
I STILL LOVE YOU
TELL ME WHAT YOU SAID AGAIN
'CAUSE I'VE BEEN FEELING DOWN AGAIN
I KNOW THAT YOU ARE TALKING
BUT I JUST CAN'T HEAR YOU TALKING

I JUST WANT TO REMIND YOU - I'LL BE STANDING BEHIND YOU
AND IF EVER YOU NEED ME - FOREVER I'LL BE THERE FOR YOU
YOU CAN LEAVE AND BREAK MY HEART
FORGET ABOUT THE THINGS WE'VE GOT
BUT NO MATTER WHAT YOU DO - I'M FOREVER THERE FOR YOU

YOU WAVED AND SAID I'LL MISS YOU BABE
I SAID THE SAME AND THEN YOU CALLED ME A FRIEND
BUT WORDS DON'T CHANGE A THING
AS I SIT UP ALL NIGHT WONDERING
AND TRYING TO MAKE SENSE
WHEN THERE'S NO SENSE TO MAKE - IT'S IN MY HEAD
REALITY IS FALLING DOWN - MY TEARS ARE RAIN ON BARREN GROUND
EVERYTHING I HAVE IS YOURS - WE NEVER FOUGHT WITHOUT A CAUSE
YOU ALWAYS TREATED ME SO GOOD
WE GOT ALONG LIKE NO ONE COULD

I JUST WANT TO REMIND YOU - I'LL BE STANDING BEHIND YOU
AND IF EVER YOU NEED ME - FOREVER I'LL BE THERE FOR YOU
YOU CAN LEAVE AND BREAK MY HEART
FORGET ABOUT THE THINGS WE'VE GOT
BUT NO MATTER WHAT YOU DO - I'M FOREVER THERE FOR YOU

WE ALWAYS WERE TOGETHER EVERY MOMENT WE COULD FIND
BUT WHEN I CALLED AND YOU WEREN'T THERE
I NEARLY LOST MY MIND

I JUST WANT TO REMIND YOU - I'LL BE STANDING BEHIND YOU
AND IF EVER YOU NEED ME - FOREVER I'LL BE THERE FOR YOU
YOU CAN LEAVE AND BREAK MY HEART
FORGET ABOUT THE THINGS WE'VE GOT
BUT NO MATTER WHAT YOU DO - I'M FOREVER THERE FOR YOU

(CONTINUED)

CONTINUED:

GETTING IT RIGHT
Lyrics by: Joe Silva   Music by: Joe Silva & David Gaspar

I MET A WEALTHY MAN WHO SOLD HIS FREEDOM
HE SAID HONESTY IS NOT CONFORMING - YOU MUST BE A GOOD MAN
HE BOUGHT A ROUND OF BEERS THEN SAID CUT YOUR HAIR

HOW WILL I KNOW WHEN I'M GETTING IT RIGHT

I MET A GIRL WHO SAID THEY CLOSED VIRGINIA
I TOLD MYSELF I'D TRUST NO OTHER - BUT HERE I AM BELIEVING
THAT AS SHE DROVE AROUND HER CAR BROKE DOWN

HOW WILL I KNOW WHEN I'M GETTING IT RIGHT

LIPS THAT LEAD ME ON
BELONG TO A FACE WHO SAYS LOVE'S ALWAYS STRONG
BUT SOMEWHERE IN THE MORNING SHE SENT ME HOME

HOW WILL I KNOW WHEN I'M GETTING IT RIGHT

I MET A PREACHER - HE TALKED OF MY SALVATION
HE SAID LET GO LET GOD
I TOLD HIM GOD HELPS THOSE THAT HELP THEMSELVES
HE KNOWS I'M WORKING HARD - THOUGH I HAVEN'T GOT FAR

HOW WILL I KNOW WHEN I'M GETTING IT RIGHT

FAITH WILL KEEP ME STRONG
HEALING HANDS WILL LEAD ME ALONG
I'LL WAIT UNTIL THE MORNING I'M TAKEN HOME

AND THEN I'LL KNOW THAT I WAS GETTING IT RIGHT
THAT'S WHEN I'LL KNOW THAT I WAS GETTING IT RIGHT
THAT'S WHEN I'LL KNOW THAT I WAS GETTING IT RIGHT

(CONTINUED)

CONTINUED:

CROSSES ON THE HIGHWAY
Lyrics & Music by: Joe Silva

CROSSES ON THE HIGHWAY - AS I DRIVE FROM MY DIVORCE
I'M LIKE AN OLD-TIME COWBOY
WHO'S MORE BROKEN THAN HIS HORSE
CROSSES ON THE HIGHWAY
I GUESS HER LOVE DIED ALONG THE ROAD
JUST LIKE MY FAITHFUL PICK-UP TRUCK
THAT STOPPED RUNNING WHEN THE WEATHER GOT COLD

BUT EVERY CROSS I PASS REMINDS ME THAT IT'S WAY TOO FAST
AND IT'S TIME TO FORGIVE
EVERY CROSS I PASS IS TELLING ME TO MAKE IT LAST
I'VE MORE MILES TO LIVE

CROSSES ON THE HIGHWAY - MY BEST FRIEND MADE 'EM OUT OF WOOD
BUT HE CHANGED HIS WORK WHEN HIS DADDY DIED
TO RUN THE BUSINESS LIKE HE THOUGHT HE SHOULD
CROSSES ON THE HIGHWAY
DID HE FORGET ABOUT WHAT THEY'RE FOR
WHILE HE DRIVES RIGHT PAST TO MEET MY EX
AND I'M SLEEPING ON SOMEONE'S FLOOR

BUT EVERY CROSS I PASS REMINDS ME THAT IT'S WAY TOO FAST
AND IT'S TIME TO FORGIVE
EVERY CROSS I PASS IS TELLING ME TO MAKE IT LAST
I'VE MORE MILES TO LIVE

CROSSES ON THE HIGHWAY - THE LAST ONE HAD SAMMY'S NAME
I'M NOT SURE IF THAT'S A BOY OR A GIRL
BUT IT'S SO SAD JUST THE SAME
CROSSES ON THE HIGHWAY - DID THEY HAVE LAST WORDS TO SAY
AND DID THEY KISS A LOVED-ONE
JUST BEFORE THEY DROVE AWAY

EVERY CROSS I PASS REMINDS ME THAT IT'S WAY TOO FAST
AND IT'S TIME TO FORGIVE
EVERY CROSS I PASS IS TELLING ME TO MAKE IT LAST
I'VE MORE MILES TO LIVE

(CONTINUED)

CONTINUED:

SURVIVE
Lyrics & Music by: Joe Silva

WHEN THEY LAID-OFF JOHN HE LOST HIS HOUSE
WELL THEY TOOK HIS MIDDLE-CLASS
NOW THE ONLY ROOF HIS FAMILY HAS IS UNDERNEATH THE OVERPASS
SO HE TRIES TO FIND A JOB
BUT NOW THAT HE DOESN'T HAVE A HOME
ON THE LINES THAT ASK ADDRESS AND NUMBER
JOHNNY WALKS AWAY ALONE

TO NEED IS NOT A CRIME - GIVE A LITTLE SOMETIME
WE'LL ALL - WE CAN ALL SURVIVE

NIKKI WAS YOUNG IN YEARS WHEN HER MOTHER TOOK HER TO THE BUS
WHEN SHE SAID WAIT HERE I'LL BE RIGHT BACK
BUT THEN WHO CAN YOU TRUST
NIKKI WALKS THROUGH LIFE ALONE
SHE WAS EATING INSIDE THE DUMP LAST NIGHT
BECAUSE SHE COULDN'T READ SIGNS A COP WENT MAD
A TRESPASSER SHOT ON SIGHT

TO NEED IS NOT A CRIME - GIVE A LITTLE SOMETIME
SO WE'LL ALL - WE CAN ALL SURVIVE

JOHNNY PRAYS HIS SON WILL GET BETTER
HE WIPES HIS EYES
THEY'RE UP AGAINST THE WINTER WEATHER
THE BOY GETS COLD AND DIES

WELL THEY STAND ON LAUREL CANYON HOLDING SIGNS UP IN THE AIR
THEY'RE SAYING HELP ME PLEASE - I'M WILLING TO WORK
THE GOVERNMENT CUT MY SHARE

TO NEED IS NOT A CRIME - GIVE A LITTLE SOMETIME
WE'LL ALL - WE CAN ALL SURVIVE

ALL SURVIVE
ALL SURVIVE
WILL ALL SURVIVE

(CONTINUED)

CONTINUED:

I DO
Lyrics & Music by: Joe Silva

YOU WALKED INTO MY ROOM - YOU UNDRESSED MY DOUBTS
NOW I BELIEVE
THAT A HEROINE PULLS A DROWNING MAN
FROM THE SEA OF DOOM TO A FAIRY-TALE

I DO

IN A WINDY PAST MY SAIL WOULD TEAR
ON NIGHTS WITHOUT A MOON
YOU'RE THE FIRST LIGHT OF A DAWNING
COME SHOW ME AFTERNOON
IF YOU LET ME GO IN A THOUSAND YEARS - NO - DON'T
FOR THAT'S TOO SOON
TWO HEARTS MAKE ONE EVOLVING
AND I THINK IT'S TRUE - ETERNAL LOVE

I DO

IF I WAS ACTING THE PLAY OF CUPID I'D FORGET MY PART
OR WORE A MASK LIKE HALLOWEEN
WOULDN'T I BE TALKING TO GHOSTS
I CAN SEE THAT YOU'RE NOT

I WOULD PRAY FOR LOVE WHEN I FELT MY HEART WAS AN EMPTY TOMB
THEN YOU APPEAR JUST LIKE AN ANGEL
DO YOU BELIEVE IN GOD
WHEN YOU SEE MIRACLES - IN YOU

I DO

CONTINUED:

BREAK THE CHAIR
Lyrics & Music by: Joe Silva

I'M SURE NOBODY FOLLOWED ME HERE
AT LEAST NO ONE REAL
AND I CLIMB THE STAIRS
THE CALL GIRL LIVING DOWN THE HALL
LONGS FOR LOVE AND TO SOMEDAY BE A MOTHER
HOW SHE EXPLAINS HER FEARS
I MADE MY BED - MAKE MY BODY NUMB TO LAY THERE
IF THEY WANT TO SIT AND TALK AS IF THEY CARE
I BREAK THE CHAIR

I TOLD HER HOW I LOVED BEFORE
AND THOUGH IT WASN'T ALWAYS PERFECT
I NEVER THOUGHT TO LEAVE
I THOUGHT THAT WE WOULD WORK THINGS OUT
SOME SAID I'M BETTER OFF WITHOUT HER
BUT WHO SHOULD I BELIEVE
FOR I SIT ALONE IN THIS SINGLE ROOM APARTMENT
WHERE THE CEILING DRIPS COMPETE AGAINST MY TEARS
UNTIL I BREAK THE CHAIR

THE SHATTERED GLASS IN THE HALL THIS MORNING
MADE IT COLD LIKE A WARNING
THAT WE ALL HAVE OUR CROSSES TO BEAR
AND ON THE STREET
ANOTHER NEIGHBOR THROWS THEIR TRASH OUT
THE GARBAGE MAN LOOKS UP AT ME IN A STARE
ANOTHER BROKEN CHAIR

SOMEONE NEW MOVES IN TODAY
I WONDER WHAT THEY'LL FEEL WHEN THEY CLIMB THE STAIRS

(CONTINUED)

CONTINUED:

THE WORD BELIEVE
Lyrics & Music by: Joe Silva

THE SKY WAS GRAY
THE WIND HOWLED AS YOU WENT AWAY
DID IT DARE SAY EVEN YESTERDAY
WASN'T MADE FOR YOU AND ME
FORGET SENSIBLE
WHILE I LAY HERE INDEFENSIBLE
AND THE WORLD GOES ONE DIMENSIONAL
AS I FLOAT RIGHT OFF THE SEA
YOU AND I BELIEVED IN CHILDHOOD
THAT IT WOULD ALWAYS BE
BUT THE WORD BELIEVE IS SPELLED WITH L-I-E

YOU WERE FIRST IN CLASS
WHEN IT CAME TO MAKING PEOPLE LAUGH
IT'S WHAT THEY WROTE UPON YOUR EPITAPH
IT'S WHAT I THINK ABOUT WHEN I GRIEVE
YOU AND I BELIEVED IN LIVING
THAT WE WOULD ALWAYS BE
BUT THE WORD BELIEVE IS SPELLED WITH L-I-E

NOW THAT YOU'RE FREE
I REMEMBER WHAT YOU SAID TO ME
IF YOU GET THE CHANCE TO FLY DON'T WAIT UP FOR ME
THEN HID YOUR PAIN UNDER YOUR SLEEVE
YOU AND I BELIEVED IN HEAVEN
THIS I STILL BELIEVE
AND THAT GOD WAS THERE AND IT'S YOU THAT HE JUST RECEIVED

THE SKY WAS GRAY
THE WIND HOWLED AS YOU WENT AWAY

(CONTINUED)

CONTINUED:

MRS. BARKER
Lyrics & Music by: Joe Silva

AT SEVEN O'CLOCK IN THE MORNING
THERE'S A RAVEN AT MRS. BARKER'S DOOR
THE KIDS TELL TALES OF MRS. BARKER'S SKELETONS
INSIDE ON THE SOFA SITS A LONELY GHOST WHO WANTS TO TALK
BUT OUTSIDE IN HER YARD THOSE TREES ARE POISONOUS
THE WINDOW OPENS - THE KIDS SAY SHHHHH
THE RAVEN TAKES A BITE
OF AN APPLE BLACK AS COAL THAT MRS. BARKER HOLDS
WE ALL KNOW MRS. BARKER
BUT WHO'S GONNA RING HER DOORBELL
IF SHE SEES YOU RUN AWAY SHE'S GONNA CAST HER SPELL
POOR OLD MRS. BARKER ARE YOU WELL
POOR OLD MRS. BARKER ARE YOU WELL

THE SUN IS GETTING HIGHER
THE RAVEN SITS ON A TELEPHONE WIRE
DARING ALL THE KIDS BELOW TO THROW STONES
THE PORCH CAT IS GONNA HISS
IF IN WALKS THE MAN WITH THE GROCERY LIST
SO HE KEEPS THE CHANGE
AND LEAVES SOME BAGS ON THE FRONT STEPS
THE DOOR OPENS - THE KIDS SAY SHHHHH
SHE LOOKS UP IN THE SKY
EVEN THE SUN SNUCK AWAY AS SHE DRAGS THE BAGS INSIDE
WE ALL KNOW MRS. BARKER
BUT WHO'S GONNA RING HER DOORBELL
WE'D ALL LIKE TO HELP HER BUT WOULD WE LIVE TO TELL
POOR OLD MRS. BARKER ARE YOU WELL
POOR OLD MRS. BARKER ARE YOU WELL

AT SEVEN O'CLOCK THIS MORNING
NO RAVEN CAME TO BARKER'S DOOR
THE KIDS TELL TALES OF MRS. BARKER LAYING THERE
THE GROCERY MAN HAD NO BAGS IN HIS HANDS
THE KIDS STARED IN A DAZE
AS THE RAVEN IN THE SKY JUST CIRCLED AROUND THE PLACE
WE ALL KNEW MRS. BARKER
BUT WHO'S GONNA RING HER DOORBELL
WE'D ALL LIKE TO HELP HER BUT WOULD WE LIVE TO TELL
POOR OLD MRS. BARKER ARE YOU WELL
POOR OLD MRS. BARKER ARE YOU WELL

(CONTINUED)

CONTINUED:

IF TODAY
Lyrics & Music by: Joe Silva

IF TODAY YOU FORGOT
THAT I WOULD DIE FOR YOU HERE ON THE SPOT
I'LL WRITE DOWN YOUR NAME AND "I LOVE YOU"
DIPPING MY PEN IN THE BLOOD OF MY HEART

IF TODAY YOU WERE GONE
IT'S A SHAME THAT IN VAIN I WAS BORN
WEAVING WOOL FOR THE EYES OF A STRANGER
WITH THE THREADS OF MY TAPESTRY TORN
THEN TOMORROW I CAN'T FIND A DAWN

IF TODAY YOU GREW UP
LEAVING ME HERE AS A CHILD
PLAYING HOUSE PRETENDING YOU'RE WITH ME
BUT MAKING BELIEVE GETS OLD AFTER A WHILE
THEN TOMORROW I CAN'T FIND A SMILE

ROSE TINTED GLASSES WILT IN FLAMES OF PASSION I KNOW
BUT HOW CAN YOU SEE DOUBLE WHERE I SEE ONE IN A ROW

IF TODAY FELL APART
HOURS FELL OFF OF A CLOCK
MINUTES SWEEP INTO PILES OF SECONDS
IF CALLING YOU MINE IS SOMETHING YOU'RE NOT
THEN TOMORROW IS NOTHING I'VE GOT
IF TODAY

CONTINUED:

LETTERS FROM WAR
Lyrics & Music by: Joe Silva

WELL YOU WROTE THAT YOU ARE SCARED
BABY I'M SCARED TOO
I TRIED TO STOP A FRIEND FROM DYING
THE BLOOD JUST SOAKED RIGHT THROUGH
THIS WAR'S BEEN SO DAMNED LONG
I STOPPED COUNTING DAYS
WHAT HELPS ME FACE ANOTHER
ARE PICTURES OF YOU I SAVE
BUT YOU'RE MILES AWAY BRINGING UP OUR CHILD ALONE
BEING AWAY FROM YOU LIKE THIS
IS THE HARDEST THING I'VE EVER KNOWN
BUT I'M THINKING OF WHEN WE'LL BE TOGETHER AGAIN SO

BABY DON'T START CRYING
YOUR STRENGTH IS WHAT I NEED THE MOST
PROMISE ME YOUR EYES ARE DRYING
TELL JUNIOR THAT DADDY LOVES YOU BOTH

MOM WHEN I WAS YOUNG
THE WAR WAS VIETNAM
YOU TAUGHT ME HOW TO PRAY
SO THEY MIGHT COME BACK UNHARMED
BUT I'VE GROWN UP MOM - IT'S MY TURN
SAY ONE MORE FOR ME
WHILE I'M FIGHTING
FOR MY FAMILY - FRIENDS - AND MY DIGNITY
MOM I NEVER LIED - I NEVER STOLE
BUT IF I TAKE A SOLDIER'S LIFE WOULD GOD FORGIVE MY SOUL
WHEN ALL THROUGH LIFE YOU TAUGHT ME RIGHT

MOTHER DON'T START CRYING
I'M TRYING HARD TO MAKE YOU PROUD
YOU USED TO SAY, "WHEN TIMES ARE TRYING
A BRIGHT SUN WILL CLEAR THESE PASSING CLOUDS"
SO BE STRONG NOW

(CONTINUED)

CONTINUED:

LET IT GO
Lyrics & Music by: Joe Silva

WHAT CAN WE SAY ABOUT TIME WE'RE WASTING
OR THE HISTORY THAT WE'RE ERASING
IN THE AFTERMATH OF WARS AND FIRES
WE'LL HAVE ALL A SOUL DESIRES
IF ALL LET IT GO TONIGHT

I'M SICK OF DEATH BECAUSE OF RACES
OR WHICH GOD THAT A SOUL EMBRACES
I'VE GOT LAND - YOU'VE GOT WATER
WE'VE BOTH ONE WORLD - NO NEED FOR BORDER
IF ALL LET IT GO TONIGHT

FOR ONCE LET'S JUST FORGET TOMORROW
AND THE LONG AGO LOAN THAT IT BORROWED
FORGIVE AND THEN JUST KEEP ON TRYING
FRIENDS ARE FRIENDS 'TIL BOTH ARE DYING
IF ALL LET IT GO TONIGHT

IT CAN HAPPEN EVERY TIME
WHEN YOU LET YOURSELF UNWIND

A TONGUE-LASH AND A REPRIMANDING
NEITHER SIDE IS UNDERSTANDING
DO WE WANT TO LIVE LIKE THAT
IN THE END IT'S ONLY CHITTER-CHAT
IF WE ALL LET IT GO TONIGHT

FRIENDS HURT FRIENDS WITH WORDS AND GLANCES
JUST LIKE RELATIVES AND MOST ROMANCES
IT HURTS LIKE HELL WHEN YOU DISCOVER
SHE WAS CASANOVA'S LOVER
BUT ALL LET IT GO TONIGHT

IT CAN HAPPEN EVERY TIME
WHEN YOU LET YOURSELF UNWIND

ALL LET IT GO TONIGHT
IF WE ALL LET IT GO TONIGHT
IF WE ALL LET IT GO TONIGHT
IF WE ALL LET IT GO TONIGHT

IT CAN HAPPEN EVERY TIME
WHEN YOU LET YOURSELF UNWIND

29382599R00135